Civil Procedure in Malawi

Civil Procedure in Malawi

Marshal Chilenga

This book was originally published as a monograph in the International
Encyclopaedia of Laws/Civil Procedure.

General Editor: Roger Blanpain
Associate General Editor: Michele Colucci
Volume Editor: Piet Taelman

Wolters Kluwer
Law & Business

Published by:
Kluwer Law International
PO Box 316
2400 AH Alphen aan den Rijn
The Netherlands
Website: www.kluwerlaw.com

Sold and distributed in North, Central and South America by:
Aspen Publishers, Inc.
7201 McKinney Circle
Frederick, MD 21704
United States of America
Email: customer.service@aspenpublishers.com

Sold and distributed in all other countries by:
Turpin Distribution Services Ltd.
Stratton Business Park
Pegasus Drive, Biggleswade
Bedfordshire SG18 8TQ
United Kingdom
Email: kluwerlaw@turpin-distribution.com

DISCLAIMER: The material in this volume is in the nature of general comment only. It is not offered as advice on any particular matter and should not be taken as such. The editor and the contributing authors expressly disclaim all liability to any person with regard to anything done or omitted to be done, and with respect to the consequences of anything done or omitted to be done wholly or partly in reliance upon the whole or any part of the contents of this volume. No reader should act or refrain from acting on the basis of any matter contained in this volume without first obtaining professional advice regarding the particular facts and circumstances at issue. Any and all opinions expressed herein are those of the particular author and are not necessarily those of the editor or publisher of this volume.

Printed on acid-free paper.

ISBN 978-90-411-3607-7

Printed in Great Britain.

About the Author

Marshal Chilenga is a legal practitioner admitted to practice law in the Supreme Court of Appeal of Malawi and courts subordinate thereto. He was admitted on 7 November 1997 and has practised civil litigation in the courts of Malawi since then. He was admitted as a notary public in 1999.

Mr Chilenga holds a Bachelor of Laws (Honours) obtained from the University of Malawi. He is a fellow of the International Bar Association in International Business Law. He also studied with the College of Law of England and Wales in International Joint Ventures, International Arbitration Law, International Capital Markets and Loans, International Intellectual Property Law and International Commercial Law.

He has written a few articles including Dikastocracy in Malawi published in KAF Occasional Papers 2008. He is also one of the consultants currently working on a new draft Civil Procedure Law for the High Court of Malawi.

He is the senior partner of the private law practice of TF & Partners.

The practice engages in civil litigation and drafting.

He is a member of the Malawi Law Society and the International Bar Association. He takes an active part in Dispute Resolution Section of the International Bar Association.

About the Author

Table of Contents

Table of Contents

Table of Contents

Table of Contents

Table of Contents

Table of Contents

Table of Contents

General Introduction

1. Malawi became independent from Britain on 6 July 1964. Prior to that Malawi was part of the Federation of Rhodesia and Nyasaland. The Federation was instituted in 1953. Prior to 1953, Nyasaland was governed by the British under the Nyasaland Order. In Council as a British Protectorate. Nyasaland became a British Protectorate in 1889.[1] Malawi therefore has inherited British common law and statutes.[2] Malawi was a one party state from 1964 up to 1994.[3] Following a successful referendum on 14 May 1993, Malawi held the first multiparty election in 1993. Malawi has population of about 13 million. It has been a member of the Southern African Development Community (SADC) since and a member of the Common Market for Eastern and Southern Africa (COMESA) since 1994. Malawi has also been a member of the African Union since 1964 and a member of the United Nations.

1. African Order in Council 1889.
2. British Central African Order in Council 1902 Art. 15.
3. Constitution of Malawi 1966 s. 4.

2. Malawi possesses a democratic multiparty Government. The President of the Republic is elected by a direct ballot together with his/her running-mate, every five years. The first President was Dr H. Kamuzu Banda who led the Country to independence. He ruled the Country from 1964 to 1994. The first government was unitary and autocratic.

3. He was followed by Bakili Muluzi who was the first multiparty President from 1994 up to 2004. Dr Bingu wa Mutharika was elected President in 2004 and he has been recently elected for a five-year term. The President can secure a maximum term of office, of five years. There are a number of political parties in the country and the notable ones include the Democratic People's Party (DPP) formed in 2004, Malawi Congress Party (MCP) formed in 1959, United Democratic Front (UDF) formed in 1993 and Alliance for Democracy (AFORD) formed in 1993.

4. Malawi is a unitary state and has no federal structures. However, the government has divided the country into three regions for administrative purposes that is, North, Centre and South. The Government has some regional offices that is, Police, Courts etc. There are tasks which are carried at a regional level. There are four High Court Registries in Malawi based in Regional structures that is, Mzuzu in the North, Lilongwe in the centre, Zomba in the East and Blantyre in the South.

5. There is a local government system in the districts. Malawi has twenty-nine districts, and each district has its own assembly which carries out development and administrative programmes. The assemblies are headed by elected representatives designated as either mayors or chairpersons, and. Administratively the assemblies are run by Chief Executives and District Commissioners, who are appointed by the Central Government. The assemblies collect local taxes and levy rates in their areas for their own administration. The Central Government funds the Local Government Finance Committee which eventually funds the assemblies. Assemblies are responsible for education, health and other social services. There is some autonomy in the assemblies. There are four cities in Malawi that is, Blantyre, Zomba, Lilongwe and Mzuzu. Freedom of worship is guaranteed in Malawi. The majority of Malawians are Christians but there is a sizeable Moslem population along the shores of Lake Malawi and the neighbouring Districts.[1] However, the state is a secular one.

1. Population Housing Census 2008.

6. The Country employs English as the official language and Chichewa is widely spoken. There are other languages that are widely spoken and these include Tumbuka, Yao, Sena, Ngonde, Alhomwe etc. The other vernacular languages are used for instruction in elementary and primary schools only, but Chichewa is examinable in schools in Malawi and there have been calls to make it a national language. However in the era of Dr Banda, use of local languages was discouraged in order to prevent tribalism, which was regarded as a threat to national unity. All bills and laws are written in English.

7. Malawi has a population of about 13 million. The population is multi- tribal and racial. The majority of the population are the Chewa, then Yao, Ahlomwe's, Tumbukas, Ngonde then Tongas and other tribes. The various tribes use their own languages and have their own cultures.

8. The Constitution of Malawi provides for three separate areas of government; that is, the Executive, the Legislature and the Judicature. The Executive companies comprise the President and his/her cabinet. It is headed by the President. The Legislature is headed by the Speaker. It comprises 193 elected members of the National Assembly and the President. The Judiciary comprises the Judges of the Supreme Court of Appeal, Judges of the High Court, Magistrates and the Chairperson of the Industrial Relations Court. The three branches of Government are independent and have checks and balances. The three branches of government also have separate and distinct rules. The Executive is responsible for the formulation and implementation of policy,[1] the Legislature, for making laws,[2] and the Judiciary, for the interpretation of the law.[3] The three arms of Government are complimentary. The High Court and Supreme Court of Appeal have constitutional control of the functioning of the government. This role was assumed in 1994.

1. Section 7 of the Constitution of Malawi.
2. Section 8 of the Constitution of Malawi.
3. Section 9 of the Constitution of Malawi.

9. Malawi is a former British Protectorate which gained its independence from the British in 1964.Malawi, then Nyasaland, become a British Protectorate in 1889 by virtue of the African Order in Council.[1] Section 13 of the Order in Council provided that the consular courts shall use the principles and substance of English law. In 1902, another British Central Africa Order in Council relating only to British Central Africa was passed, which preserved the statutes of general application, English common law and the doctrine of equity, as applicable law, as of 11 August 1902,.[2]

1. African Order In Council 1889.
2. Article 15.

10. Prior to 1889 the people in British Central Africa were governed by customary law. In the colonial era, the customary law that was preserved was only what was not repugnant to justice and morals or repugnant to natural justice, equity and good conscience. Section 20 of the British Central Africa Order in Council[1] provided that every court, including the High Court, in all cases civil and criminal, to which parties were natives, 'shall be guided by customary law so far as it is practicable and not repugnant to justice and morality and is not inconsistent with any Order in Council or Ordinance or any regulation or rule made under any Order in Council or Ordinance'. Customary law, being unwritten, was difficult to ascertain, and it needed to be proved as fact in evidence before being accepted by the courts. Customary law was limited in application, as each community had its own laws. There was no uniformity, hence customary law preserved ethnicity. It was preserved in areas of marriage and succession. The courts at custom were arbitral and reconciliatory in nature. They were run by village, kindred or associational courts where there was persuasion of and consent among the disputants rather than force and compulsion. The role of the supernatural affected customary law greatly in areas of land tenure, family organization and governance, succession and inheritance, definition of crime and investigation and decision of charges. Local courts, as opposed to consular courts, applied customary law in the colonial period.

1. British Central African Order in Council 1902.

11. In 1889, the African Order in Council created a parallel court system that is, the local and consular courts. The system was preserved by the Subordinate Courts Ordinance 1906. The Courts Ordinance 1929 continued the application of customary law courts up to 1933. In 1933, the Native Courts Ordinance was passed. The Ordinance created native authorities as heads of the local courts. In 1961, the Local Courts Act was passed, changing the structure of the courts.

12. In 1962, the local courts were subjected to the control of a minister who was a member of the executive arm of the Government. The Native authority was removed from his previous role as head of the local court. However the Local Court (Amendment Act) 1969 was the most retrogressive and oppressive amendment. The local courts became endowed with jurisdiction over serious crimes like murder and treason. The courts then became instruments of repression. In 1994, the courts were suspended but the Traditional Courts Act[1] has not yet been repealed. Arguably, these courts may be resuscitated. Attempts have been made to reintroduce local courts with limited civil jurisdiction, after 1994, but no result has been seen yet.

1. Cap 3.03 of the Laws of Malawi.

13. The British Central Africa Order in Council continued till 1961 when the Nyasaland Constitution Order in Council[1] was passed. It preserved section 15 of the British Central Africa Order in Council. The Nyasaland Order in Council Amendments No. 2 did not state the cut off date of the received statutes. However, the Malawi Independence Order 1964 reproduced section 15 of the British Central Africa Order in Council 1902, which provided for the application of the statutes of general application, English common law and the doctrine of equity. The Constitution Act 1966, section 15, preserved the application of the existing laws, the substance of common law and the doctrine of equity. Section 2 of the Constitution Act defined existing laws as all Acts, Orders in Council, laws, rules, regulations, resolutions, orders or other instruments having the effect of law in any part of Malawi before the appointed day. This preserved the statutes of general application in England as of 11 August 1902. The applicable laws have been preserved by section 210 of the Republic of Malawi Constitution.

1. British Central Africa Order in Council 1907.

Chapter 1. Judicial System

§1. The Courts

14. There is a one Court system in Malawi which is known as High Court (sic) system. The system comprises the Supreme Court of Appeal, High Court of Malawi and Magistrate Courts.[1] Prior to 1994, the country had a Traditional Court[2] system which operated parallel to the High Court system.

  1. Section 103(3) of the Constitution of the Republic of Malawi.
  2. These courts were established under the Traditional Courts Act cap 3:03 of the Laws of Malawi which is still law but has its operation suspended by the coming into force of the Constitution in 1994.

15. The Judiciary was established under section 103(3) of the Constitution of the Republic of Malawi.[1] It is provided that there shall be no courts established of superior or concurrent jurisdiction with the Supreme Court of Appeal, or the High Court. The Supreme Court of Appeal shall be the highest appellate Court and shall have jurisdiction to hold such powers as may be conferred on it by this Constitution or any other law. The Supreme Court of Appeal has jurisdiction to hear appeals from the High Court and such other courts and tribunals as an Act of Parliament may prescribe.[2] The court also hears appeals from the Court Martial established under the Defence Act.[3]

  1. Malawi adopted a new Constitution which came into force on 18 May 1994 after Presidential and Parliamentary Elections were held.
  2. Section 104(2) of the Constitution of the Republic of Malawi.
  3. Defence Act cap 12;01 of the Laws of Malawi.

§2. The High Court of Malawi

16. The High Court of Malawi is created under section 108 of the Constitution with unlimited original jurisdiction to hear and determine any civil or criminal proceedings under any law. The High Court has the power to review any law and any decision of the Government for conformity with the Constitution, under section 108(2) of the Constitution.[1] There has been the emergence of two divisions of the High Court in Malawi, namely, the Constitutional Court[2] and the Commercial Court.[3]

  1. Section 5 of the Constitution of the Republic of Malawi has been used as a forum for reviewing the constitutionality of laws and acts of Government in Malawi.
  2. Section 9 of the Courts Act was amended to provide for hearing of constitutional matters before a panel of three judges.On appeal a panel of five judges would preside over the matter.
  3. The court was set up administratively by the Chief Justice promulgating High Court (Commercial Division) Rules 2007.

§3. MAGISTRATE'S COURTS

17. Magistrate courts are subordinate courts to the High Court of Malawi. These Courts are presided over by professionals and lay magistrates. These courts are established under section 110(1) of the Constitution.

§4. INDUSTRIAL RELATIONS COURT

18. This Court is subordinate to the High Court. It is a specialized court dealing with labour disputes and such other matters relating to employment. This court is established under section 110(2) of the Constitution of the Republic of Malawi. It is operationalized by the Labour Relations Act.[1]

1. Section 63 of the Labour Relations Act cap 54:01 of the Laws of Malawi as read with s. 110(2) of the Constitution of the Republic of Malawi.

§5. TRADITIONAL COURTS

19. These courts are not operational currently. Section 110(3) of the Constitution provides for traditional or local courts presided over by lay chiefs, with limited jurisdiction.[1] The jurisdiction is limited exclusively to civil cases, minor common law offences, and statutory offences as prescribed by an Act of Parliament.

1. There is an attempt by the Law Commission to revive the traditional courts in conformity with the Constitution as these courts have been in operational since 1994.

Chapter 2. Sources of Law

§1. SOURCES OF LAW

20. The sources of law include Acts of Parliament and subsidiary legislation (i.e., regulations and rules) and decided cases.

§2. SUPREME COURT OF APPEAL

Diagrammatically the Malawi Court system is as follows:-

Supreme Court of Appeal

High Court of Malawi

|

Magistrate Courts – Industrial Relations Court

21. The main source of civil procedure in the Malawi Supreme Court of Appeal is the Supreme Court of Appeal Act.[1] Section 8 of the Supreme Court of Appeal Act provides as follows:

> The practice of the Supreme Court of Appeal shall be in accordance with this Act and any rules made thereunder:
> Provided that if this Act or any rules of Court made thereunder does not make provision for any particular point of practice and procedure then the practice and procedure of the Court shall be:-
> (b) in relation to civil matters as may be in accordance with the law and practice for the time being observed by the Court of Appeal in England.

1. Cap 3;01 of the Laws of Malawi.

22. In *Wilson Pillane v. Commercial Union,*[1] it was held that the Malawi Supreme Court of Appeal Rules apply in the Malawi Supreme Court of Appeal. The sources of procedure are thus the Act, Rules of the Supreme Court (RSC) in England, and decided cases.

1. [1994] MLR 263 (MSCA).

§3. HIGH COURT

23. Section 29 of the Courts Act[1] stipulates the rules of procedure in the following manner:

Save as otherwise provided in this Act, the practice and procedure of the High Court shall so far as local circumstances admit, shall be the practice and procedure (including the practice and procedure relating to execution provided in the Rules of the Supreme Court 1999):

Provided that-

(a) the Rules of the Supreme Court may at any time be varied, supplemented, revoked or replaced by rules of court made under this Act;

(b) any of the Rules of the Supreme Court which refer solely to procedure under Acts of the U.K. Parliament other than the statutes of general application in force in England on the eleventh day of August 1902 and any such Acts as have been applied from time to time and are in force in Malawi shall not have any application in Malawi;

(c) If any provision of the Rules of the Supreme Court is inconsistent with any provision of any rules of Court, the latter shall prevail and the Rules of the Supreme Court shall to the extent of such inconsistency, be void.

1. Cap 3:02 of the Laws of Malawi.

24. Section 29 was wrongly amended, as the rules applicable were the rules in force in England in 1965. There were no new Supreme Court Rules in 1999 in England, only an edition of the Supreme Court Practice.

25. Local circumstances did not permit the application of Order 77 of the RSC made under Crown Proceedings Act 1947 in *Emma Sisya v. Attorney General[1993] 2 MLR820*. The Crown Proceedings Act 1947 is inapplicable in Malawi.

26. In *Anwar Gani v. Chande,*[1] The Malawi Supreme Court of Appeal held that Order 59 of the RSC was inconsistent with Rule 5 of the High Court (Exercise of Jurisdiction of Registrar) Rules. The English rules were held to be inapplicable in Malawi.

1. MSCA 6 of 2003.The case overruled *Banda v. Chunga* [1990] 13 MLR 53, which had been law since 1990.It was only overruled in 2006.

27. Further, there is currently a practical problem as England changed its rules of civil procedure in 1999 by adopting Civil Procedure Rules.[1] In Malawi, section 29 was amended in 2004 in order to adopt the RSC of England 1999, though these were discarded in England as being applicable rules. This change has negatively affected the rules of practice in Malawi as there is no further update on the previous rules in England. Attempts have been made to draft Civil Procedure Rules for Malawi and the drafting process is currently ongoing.[2] There is hope that new Civil Procedure Rules may be promulgated soon. The review and drafting of the rules is currently in progress. In *Maunde v. National Bank of Malawi,*[3] changes to the procedure in England made the application of the rules in Malawi difficult. England had changed its 1979 White Book in 1982, which was held to be inapplicable in Malawi.

1. The Woolf Report 1998.
2. Draft Civil Procedure Rules 2008 are available.
3. 10 MLR 360.

§4. SUBORDINATE COURTS

28. Section 59 of the Courts Act stipulates that:

Without prejudice to section 67, the Chief Justice may make rules of Court
(a) regulating the pleading, practice and procedure to be followed in subordinate courts in all causes and matters whatsoever or with respect to which subordinate courts have for the time being jurisdiction, and all matters incidental or relating to any such pleading, practice and procedure, including the manner in which and time within which any application under any law for the time being in force are to be made;
(b) regulating the costs and charges to be allowed and the fees to be payable in respect of proceedings in any subordinate court;
(c) regulating the procedure in connection with the transfer of any proceedings from any subordinate court to the High Court or from the High Court to any subordinate court;
(d) regulating the means by which particular facts may be proved and the mode in which evidence thereof may be given in any proceedings or on any application in connection with or at any stage of proceedings;
(e) amending the Rules of Court made under the British Central Africa Order in Council,1902;
(f) prescribing anything which under this Part ,is to be done or may be prescribed;
(g) generally for the better carrying out of this Part

29. The Chief Justice has made subordinate court Rules. Such Rules shall not be a subject of this discussion at all.

§5. INDUSTRIAL RELATIONS COURT RULES

30. These rules have been made under the Labour Relations Act. The Rules have been made by the Chief Justice. These rules shall not be subject of this discussion save for a discussion on conduct of appeals.

§6. CONSTITUTIONAL COURT RULES

31. Section 9 of the Courts Act[1] has introduced a Constitutional Division of the High Court. The division has its own rules. These rules provide for the filing of skeleton arguments within fourteen days before the date of hearing. Each party needs to prepare six sets of documents and file the same with the court and serve them on the other party. The hearing takes place before a panel of three judges, and on appeal a minimum of five judges shall sit on the bench.

1. Cap 3:02 of the Laws of Malawi.

§7. COMMERCIAL COURT RULES

32. A commercial Division of the High Court has been established. It has special rules which are similar to the general Rules in the High Court. These Rules will be discussed generally.

33. The focus of the monograph will be the practice and procedure in the High Court of Malawi.

§8. INTERNATIONAL LAW IN MALAWI

34. International law has been recognized in Malawi as part of its operating law. Section 211 of the Constitution of the Republic of Malawi provides that:

(1) Any international agreement ratified by an Act of Parliament shall form part of the law of the Republic if so provided for in the Act of Parliament ratifying the agreement.
(2) International agreements entered into before the commencement of this Constitution and binding on the Republic shall form part of the law of the Republic, unless Parliament subsequently provides otherwise or the agreement otherwise lapses.
(3) Customary international law, unless inconsistent with his Constitution or an Act of Parliament, shall have continued application.

35. The applicable international laws are treaties and customary international laws. The notable treaties in Malawi include the United Nations Charter, the African Union Charter, the African Commission Charter on peoples and Human Rights, the SADC Treaty and the Southern COMESA.

36. By virtue of the African Charter, Malawians are subject to the jurisdiction of the African Commission that sits in Banjul. There are further appeals to Banjul on human rights issues after exhaustion of local remedies in Malawi.

37. The COMESA Court whose seat is in Sudan has jurisdiction over trade disputes. There is thus an extended territorial jurisdiction by virtue of the COMESA Treaty.

38. The SADC treaty has created the SADC Tribunal which sits in Windhoek, Namibia. This treaty has subjected Malawian citizens to a wider tribunal after the exhaustion of local remedies.

39. Malawi has signed but not yet ratified the Rome Convention on the International Criminal Court hence it would not be subject to that Tribunal yet. However, Malawi is subject to the World Trade Organization and other United Nations Tribunals.

40. Malawi is part of the global village and the treaties evidence the fact. Malawi is thus bound by customary international law and general principles of law.

§9.   THE LEGAL PROFESSION

41.   The legal profession in Malawi is like most law, based on the English model. But there is no division between barristers and solicitors. Malawi has legal practitioners in its fused system.

42.   Trials in the Magistrate Courts proceed without legal practitioners. Very few peoples are represented in Malawi. Most individuals conduct their own cases in the Magistrate and Industrial Relations Court. However in the High Court, there is need for legal representation and lawyers are always engaged. In the Malawi Supreme Court of Appeal, it is compulsory for litigants to engage lawyers. The complication and sophistication of the procedures in the High Court and Malawi Supreme Court make legal representation a must. However, parties are at liberty to present their own cases in person without the aid of a legal practitioner at all stages. The right to legal representation is one of the fundamental rights. In criminal cases it is compulsory, and the state is obliged to provide representation where one cannot afford it.[1]

   1.   Section 42 of the Republic of Malawi Constitution.

43.   The minimum qualification for a legal practitioner in Malawi is a Bachelor of Laws (Honours) Degree from the University of Malawi. The law recognizes qualifications from some countries with either common law or Roman-Dutch traditions.[1] The law would most to ascertain the minimum courses of study. The qualifications are scrutinized by the Malawi Council for Legal Education. The Council comprises the Attorney General, a Judge of the High Court, a Magistrate appointed by the Chief Justice, two persons in legal service in Government, the registered legal practitioners nominated by Malawi Law Society and appointed by the Minister, and two law teachers appointed by the Minister.

   1.   Section 9, Legal Education and Legal Practitioner's Act.

44.   The Council has a number of functions to perform and these include:[1]

(a)   To make regulations for the syllabus and curriculum of legal education and for attendance at law school(s).
(b)   To establish, conduct and regulations of legal education.
(c)   To conduct, regulate and control the holding of examinations in law.
(d)   To advise and recommend to the Minister on matters relating to legal education and the necessary qualifications for admission and enrolment of legal functions.
(e)   To perform such other functions and deal with such other matters relating to legal education as the Minister may deal with, in writing.

   1.   Section 9.

45.   Admission to practice law in Malawi as upon the fulfilment of certain qualifications, that is, he/she is a citizen of Malawi or must have resided in Malawi for a continuous period of three months immediately before filing the petition for admission, holds a degree or diploma in law from a prescribed institution or has been admitted to practice law as a barrister, solicitor, signet or attorney in a specified country, has set and passed the Malawi law examinations, or obtained the Degree of Bachelor of Laws (Honours) from the University of Malawi.[1] Persons employed by the Malawi Government may be admitted as officers and legal practitioners.[2]

    1. Section 11, Legal Education and Legal Practitioner's Act.
    2. Section 21, Legal Education and Legal Practitioner's Act.

46. In a number of circumstances, the High Court may make an order suspending or striking a legal practitioner off the rolls, or may admonish him/her.[1] The High Court may act on its own motions or on a complaint. The legal practitioner may be disciplined on engaging in unprofessional conduct, for example, fraud, overcharging, dishonesty, conviction for a term of twelve months, bringing the profession to disrepute,[2] etc.

    1. Section 21, Legal Education and Legal Practitioner's Act.
    2. Section 21, Legal Education and Legal Practitioner's Act.

47. All legal practitioners admitted to practice law in Malawi are members of the Malawi Law Society.[1] The Society regulates its own conduct through the Disciplinary Committee.[2] The Society also has a code of Ethics to regulate the conduct of legal practitioners.[3] The Law Society guarantees independence of the profession.

    1. Section 27, Legal Education and Legal Practitioner's Act.
    2. Section 37, Legal Education and Legal Practitioner's Act.
    3. The Code was made under s. 36 of the Legal Education and Legal Practitioner's Act.

§10. LEGAL AID

48. Legal Aid in Malawi is available for deserving persons in criminal and Civil Cases. In criminal cases, the Constitution provides the right to legal aid.[1] However practically, it is not guaranteed due to shortage of personnel. There are three legal aid offices operating in the country with a population of 13 million. There are less than ten legal aid advocates in Malawi; hence it is impossible to have an effective legal aid scheme. The decision on whether or not to grant legal aid may be made by the Chief Legal Aid Advocate or the Magistrate Court or the High Court Judge.[2] A fee may be paid to the Legal Aid Department before representation is provided. The Chief Legal Aid Advocate may retain private legal practitioners to conduct any matter.[3]

    1. Section 42 of the Republic of Malawi Constitution.
    2. Legal Aid Act cap 4:01 of the Laws of Malawi ss 4, 5, 6 and 7.
    3. Section 13, Legal Aid Act.

Chapter 3. Stages of Proceedings

§1. The Main Stages in High Court Proceedings

49. The main stages in civil proceedings commenced by way of writ of summons include:

(a)   Issue of originating process.
(b)   Service of originating process.
(c)   Service of pleadings.
(d)   Directions for trial.
(e)   Discovery of documents.
(f)   Listing for trial.
(g)   Trial.
(h)   Taxing of costs.
(i)   Execution.
(j)   Appeals.

50. There are separate stages for other proceedings like originating summons, judicial review and petitions which will be discussed separately.

§2. Issue of Process

51. Court proceedings are commenced by issuing an originating process. This includes drawing up an appropriate document, taking it to the court office, paying a fee and having the originating process stamped with the court's official seal. The documents are normally drawn up by a legal practitioner throughout the litigation process. All limited companies are supposed to be legally represented by a legal practitioner in Malawi, according to *Munthali v. United Bus Transport Company Ltd.*[1] Some processes may be issued by litigants in person. The originating process falls into four categories (1)

1.   7MLR 438.

52. Writ of summons (2) Originating summons (3) Originating Motion and (4) Petition. These will be discussed later.

§3. Service of Process

53. As a general rule, the originating process must be served on the defendant within four months after issue of the process. The responsibility to serve the process remains on the plaintiff. There are a number of ways of serving the process and these include advertisement in the press.

§4. Pleadings

54. In common law actions, the factual contentions of the parties must be reduced to writing, in formal documents known as 'pleadings'. The first pleading is drawn up by the Plaintiff and it known as a statement of claim. This pleading sets out the facts establishing the plaintiff's causes of action against the defendant.

55. The second pleading is the defence which is drawn up by the defendant. It responds to the allegations made in the statement of claim and sets up specific defences available to the defendant. A defendant with a cross-claim against the plaintiff may add a counterclaim to the defence. The plaintiff may then serve a reply to the defence and the defence will get to counterclaim.

§5. Directions for trial

56. Normally after closure of pleadings, the High Court will give directions for trial. The court will give directions as to the date, place, mode of trial, and exchange of witness statements. Currently, directions will only be given after there has been an attempt to resolve the matter by way of mediation. Directions will only be given if there is a certificate from a mediator stating that mediation has failed.

§6. Discovery

57. After the close of the pleadings, the parties are required to serve on each other lists of documents verified by affidavits. These include a list of the documents material to the case which are or have been in their possession, custody or power. All documents need to be disclosed, whether they support or undermine a party's case. After the exchange of lists parties are at liberty to inspect each other's documents and may make copies. However, some documents are privileged from disclosure and these may not be subjected to disclosure.

§7. Listing for trial

58. When parties have complied with all directions for trial, the parties will set down the action for trial by lodging the necessary bundles. The plaintiff must prepare a bundle of pleading, a court bundle which must contain witness statements, skeleton arguments and a list of authorities.

§8. Trial

59. All witnesses will be called to give oral testimony on the facts and adduce all documents in support of their cases. The court will determine the admissibility as well as relevance of the evidence. Trials are normally conducted with a judge sitting alone in open court. There are no jury trials in civil cases in Malawi. After the hearing, counsel will make submissons to the court on the evidence and the law, and then the court will later give its judgment.

§9. TAXATION OF COSTS

60. A party given the judgment normally may receive the judgment for costs as well. The costs will be quantified and presented to the Registrar in a process called taxation.

§10. EXECUTION

61. A judgment obtained in the High Court will be useless if it cannot be enforced. The process of enforcement may include execution through the sheriff of Malawi. Most judgments of the Court are money judgments, and hence there is need for a procedure to enforce them. The modes of enforcement of judgments will be discussed later.

§11. THE INITIATIVE

62. Litigation begins with the plaintiff. The plaintiff is responsible for ensuring that the action proceeds expeditiously through its various stages. The plaintiff is said to have the courage of the matters. The defendant may also take some steps in order to exert pressure on the plaintiff, which include making payment into court, making a counterclaim, applying for security for costs, or applying to strike out or dismiss the plaintiff's claim.

Chapter 4. Commencement of Proceedings

§1. Mode of Commencement of Civil Proceedings in the High Court

63. Order 5 Rule 1 of the RSC provides that, subject to any Act and these rules, civil proceedings in the High Court may be begun by writ, originating summons, originating motion or petition.

64. There are various laws which prescribe how the proceedings may begin, that is, the Presidential and Parliamentary Elections Act[1] requires that actions be commenced by way of petitions supported by affidavit, Statute Law (Miscellaneous Provisions) Act[2] also prescribes that applications may begin by an originating summons or originating motion.

1. Cap 2:01 of the Laws of Malawi s. 115.
2. Cap 5:01 of the Laws of Malawi.

65. Order 5 Rule 2 provides that subject to any provision of an Act, or these rules, by virtue of which any proceedings are expressly required to be begin otherwise than by writ, the following proceedings must, notwithstanding anything in Rule 4, be begun by writ, that is to say proceedings:

(a) In which a claim is made by the plaintiff for any relief or remedy in tort, other than trespass to land.
(b) In which a claim made by the plaintiff is based on allegation of fraud.
(c) In which a claim is made by the plaintiff for damages for breach of duty (whether the duty exists by virtue of contract or of a person) made by or under an Act or independently of any contract or any such provision, whether the damages claimed consist of or include damages in respect of the death of any person or in respect of personal injuries to any person or in respect of damage to any property.

Generally all contentious actions must be begun by way of a writ of summons.

66. Order 5 Rule 4 of the RSC provides:

Except in the case of proceedings which by these rules or by under any Act are required to be begun by writ or originating summons or are required or authorized to be begun by originating motion or petition, proceedings may begun by either writ or originating summons as the plaintiff considers appropriate.

§2. Proceedings

(a) in which the sole or principal question at issue is or is likely to be one of construction of an Act or of any instrument made under an Act or of any deed, will, contract or other or document or some other question of law;

(b) in which there is unlikely to be any substantial dispute of fact, are appropriate to be begun by originating summons unless the plaintiff intends in those proceedings to apply for a summary judgment under Order 14 or Order 86 or if for any other reason the Court considers the proceedings more appropriate to begin by writ.

67. Order 5 Rule 5 RSC provides that proceedings may begun by originating motion if, but only if, by these rules or by or under any Act, the proceedings are required or authorized to be so begun. For example, a petition for winding up under the Companies Act.[1]

  1. Cap 46:03 of the Laws of Malawi s. 271.

68. Order 5 Rule 6 of the RSC restricts the rights of persons to sue in person in the following manner:

69. Subject to paragraph (2) and to Order 80 Rule 2, any person, whether or not he/she sues as a trustee or personal representative or in any other capacity, may begin and carry on proceedings in the High Court by a solicitor or in person.

70. Except expressly as provided by or under any enactment, a body corporate may not begin or carry on such proceedings otherwise than by a solicitor.[1]

  1. Malawi has a fused legal profession; hence the words 'solicitor' and 'legal practitioner' are used interchangeably.

71. In *UTM v. Munthali*[1] it was held that a limited company may only defend legal proceedings with the aid of a legal practitioner.

  1. *supra*

§3. WRIT OF SUMMONS – ORDER 6

72. Order 6 Rule 1 of the RSC provides that every writ shall be in form No.1 in Appendix A.

Writ appears thus:

Between

– – – – – – – – – – plaintiff

And

..........................defendant

To The Defendant [*name*]

of

THIS WRIT OF SUMMONS has been issued against you by the above-named Plaintiff in respect of the claim set out on the back.

Within [14 days] after the service of this Writ on you, counting the day of service, you must either satisfy the claim or return to the Court Office mentioned below the accompanying ACKNOWLEDGMENT OF SERVICE stating therein whether you intend to contest these proceedings.

If your fail to satisfy the claim or to return the Acknowledgment within the time stated, or if you return the Acknowledgment without stating therein an intention to contest the proceedings, the Plaintiff may proceed with the action and judgment may be entered against you forthwith without further notice.

Issued from the Central Office [or the Admiralty and Commercial Registry] [or Chancery Chambers] or

[District Registry] of the High Court this _____day of_____ 19____

Note- This writ may not be served later than 4 calendar months (*or, if leave is required to effect service out of the jurisdiction, 6 months)*beginning with that date unless renewed by order of the Court.

Important

Directions for Acknowledgment of Service are given with the accompanying form.

Back of No. 1

[Statement of Claim]

The Plaintiff' claim is for

Where words appear between square brackets delete if inapplicable

Signed if statement of claim indorsed]

[Agent for of

Solicitor for the said Plaintiff whose address is

[*or where the Plaintiff sues in person*

THIS WRIT was issued by the said Plaintiff who resides at

And (*if the Plaintiff does not reside within the jurisdiction) whose address for service is.*

73.   Every writ will be completed by the plaintiffs' legal practitioner and be issued by the Registrar or Deputy or Assistant Registrar of the High Court of Malawi.[1]

1.   Section 3 of the Courts Act cap:3:02 of the Laws of Malawi.

74. The writ must contain the titles of the parties and contain the plaintiff's address for service as well as the defendants address for service.

75. Writ of summons forms are available from the Government Print, but currently most legal houses are adapting the writ in their own forms. There has been a diminished use of the Government Printer forms with the increased use of computers and word processors, which has reduced the cost of purchasing the forms.

76. Order 6 Rule 2 provides:

(1) Before a writ is issued it must be endorsed -
 (a) with a statement of claim or if the statement of claim is not endorsed in the writ, with a concise statement of the nature of the claim made or the relief or remedy required in the action begin thereby.
 (b) where the claim made by the plaintiff is for debt or liquidated demand only with a statement of the amount claimed in respect of the debt or demand for costs and also with a statement that further proceedings will be stayed if, with the Civil Procedure Malawi time for acknowledging service, the defendant pays the amount so claimed to the plaintiff, his solicitor or agent.
 (c) where the claim made by the plaintiff is for possession of land, with a statement showing-
  (i) whether the claim relates to a dwelling house.
  (ii) if it does, whether the rateable value of the premises on every day specified by section 4 (2) of the Rent Act 1977 in relation to the premises exceed the sum so specified or whether the rent from the time being payable in respect of the premises exceeds the sum specified in section 4(4) (b) of the Rent Act 1977; and
  (iii) in a case where the plaintiff knows of any person entitled to claim relief against forfeiture as underlessee (including a mortgagee under section 146 (4) of the Law of Property Act 1925) or in accordance with section 38 of the Supreme Court 1981 the name and address of that person.
 (d) where an action is brought to enforce a right to recover possession of goods, with a statement showing the value of the goods.
 (e) where the action relates to a consumer credit agreement, with a certificate that the action is not one to which section 141 of the Consumer Credit Act applies.
 (f) where the action is an action for personal injuries with a statement that the action is not one which by virtue of article 5 of the High Court and Country Courts Jurisdiction Order 1991 must be commenced in the country court.
(2) where particulars are given pursuant to paragraph 1(c) (iii), the plaintiff must send a copy of the writ to the person named.

77. The Acts mentioned in Rule 1 are not applicable in Malawi and hence those rules are not applicable by virtue of section 29 of the Courts Act, that is, local circumstances and that the said Acts are not statutes of general application.[1]

1. Statutes of general application are statutes in force in England as of 11 Aug. 1902 which were received in British Central Africa by virtue of the British Central Africa Order in Council 1902. see Finnis JM Plain Speaking about Some Existing Laws UMA Students Law Journal 1981 at 38, Haynes CP Confusion Confounded: The Appearance of Reality *ibid* at 1, Nzunda CM A Sequel to Confusion Double Confounded; The Appearance of Reality *ibid.*, 9.

78.   Order 6 Rule 3 requires that the capacity in which the plaintiff is suing or the defendant is being sued must be endorsed on the writ.

79.   Order 6 Rule 4 requires that the place where the cause of action arose must be endorsed in the writ as well.

80.   Order 6 Rule 5 requires that the plaintiff's legal practitioner must endorse the plaintiff's address and the legal practitioner's address within Malawi. The address for service on the plaintiff is his/her legal practitioner's address. Similarly, after a defendant has acknowledged service, his/her address for service shall be his/her legal practitioner's address if he/she has one, or his/her address indicated on the form of acknowledgment.

§4. ORDER 8: ORIGINATING MOTIONS

81.   Notices of originating motions are used in certain types of proceedings which are expressly provided for by statute, procedural rural imposed by statutory instrument or rules of court governing the type of proceedings in question, for example, judicial review.

§5. THE NOTICE

82.   Under Order 8 Rule 2(1) an ex parte notice of motion may be made ex parte except where there is delay which may result in irreparable or serious mischief, and in such a case, the Court may grant the applications on such terms as to costs or undertakings, as the Court may deem just.

83.   Under Order 8(2) RSC, unless the Court gives leave to the contrary, there must be at least two clear days between the service of the notice of a motion and the day named in the notice for hearing the motion.

§6. FORM AND ISSUE OF NOTICE

84.   Order 8 Rule 3(1) provides that the notice must be in form No. 13, and where leave has been given under Rule 2(2) to serve short notice of motion, that fact must be stated in the notice.

85.   Order 8 Rules 3(2) provides that the notice must include a concise statement of the nature of the claim or relief required.

86. Under Order 8 Rule 3(6), issue of an originating motion takes place upon its being sealed by an officer of the Court out of which it is issued. In Malawi, all motions are issued by the Registrar or Deputy or Assistant Registrar of the High Court.

§7. SERVICE OF MOTION WITH WRIT

87. Order 8 Rule 4 provides that notice of a motion is to be made in an action served by the Plaintiff on the defendant, with a writ of summons or originating summons or at any time after service of such writ or summons, whether or not the defendant has acknowledged service in the action. However, it has to be noted that such notice of motion is not an originating motion, it is an interlocutory one.

88. Under Order 8 Rule 5 RSC, the hearing of any motion may be adjourned from time to time on such terms, if any, as the Court thinks fit.

§8. PETITIONS: ORDER 9

89. Petitions are used in the High Court for certain applications of bankruptcy, in relation to companies, elections and divorce, declarations of legitimacy etc. Petitions are generally governed by special rules.

90. Rules 2 to 4 apply to a petition by which civil proceedings in the High Court are begun subject, in the case of petitions of any particular class, to any special provisions relating to petitions of that class made by these Rules or under any Act.

91. The statutes on which petitions are made include the Divorce Act,[1] the Presidential and Parliamentary Elections Act[2] and the Companies Act.[3]

1. Cap 25:04 of the Laws of Malawi as read with The Matrimonial Cause Rules 1950.
2. *Supra.*
3. *Supra.*

§9. CONTENTS OF PETITION

92. Order 9 Rule 2(1) provides that every petition must have, printed or endorsed by an officer of the Court, at the head of the first page, a replica of the coat of arms and must include a concise statement of the claim made or relief or remedy required in the proceedings beginning thereby. Petitions challenging the election of a Member of Parliament under section 114 of the Presidential and Parliamentary Elections Act must be supported by an affidavit of evidence, to be filed within two days from the date of announcement of the results.

93. Order 9 Rule 2(2) provides that the petition must include a statement of the names of persons, if any, required to be served herewith, or if no person is to be served, a statement to that effect.

94. Under Order 9 Rule 4 a day and time for hearing of a petition shall be fixed by the Registrar.

95. Order 9 Rule 5 provides that there shall be no application in any cause or matter may be made by petition. However, summonses or motions may be made in an action begun by petition.

Chapter 5. Service of Process and Documents

§1. Service

96. After the originating process has been issued, it is important that the other party must be served. In Malawi, service makes a person amenable to the jurisdiction of the courts. Mere service gives power to the courts to try actions which may be inappropriate in Malawi. Conversely, if a defendant is not present in the jurisdiction, Malawi courts are denied power to try actions which would be appropriate.

97. Service under Malawian civil procedure law has been regulated by Orders 10, 11,65,80,81 and 114 of the RSC, section 137 of the Companies Act,[1] the Immunities and Privileges Act[2] and Civil Procedure (Suits By or Against Government) Act.[3]

1. *Supra.*
2. Cap 16:01 of the Laws of Malawi.
3. Cap 6:01 of the Laws of Malawi deals with service of documents and process on the Attorney General.

§2. Writ of Summons: Order 10

98. Order 10 Rules (1) of the RSC provides that a writ must be served personally on each defendant by the plaintiff or his/her agent.

99. Order 10 Rule 4(1) provides that service of a writ of summons on a defendant within the jurisdiction may, instead of being served personally on him/her, may be served:

(1) By sending a copy of the writ by ordinary first-class post to the defendant at his/her usual or last known address.
(2) If there is a letter box for that address, by inserting through the letter box a copy of the writ enclosed in a sealed envelope addressed to the defendant.

100. First-class post means first-class post which has been prepaid or in respect of which a further payment is not required.

101. Where a writ is served in accordance with paragraph (2)

102. the date of service shall, unless the contrary is shown, be deemed to be the eighth day (ignoring Order 3 Rule 5) from when it was sent to, or as the case may be, inserted through the letter box for that address in question.

103. Any affidavit proving due service of the writ must contain a statement to the effect that:

(i)   in the opinion of the deponent (or if the deponent is the plaintiff's legal practitioner or an employee of that legal practitioner, in the opinion of the plaintiff) the copy of the writ, if sent through the letter box of the address in question will have come to the knowledge of the defendant within seven days thereafter; and

(ii) in the case of service by post, the copy of the writ has not been returned to the Plaintiff as undelivered to the address.

104.   Where a defendant's legal practitioner endorses on the writ, a statement that he/she accepts services of the writ on behalf of the defendant, the writ shall be deemed to have been duly served on that defendant and to have been served on the date on which the endorsement was made.

105.   Subject to Order 12 Rule 7, where a writ is not duly served on the defendant but he/she acknowledges service of it, the writ shall be deemed, unless the contrary is shown, to have been duly served on him/her and to have been so served on the date on which he/she acknowledges service.

106.   Every copy of the writ for service on the defendant shall be sealed with the seal of the office of the High Court out of which the writ was issued, and shall be accompanied by a form of acknowledgement of service in Form No. 14 in Appendix A, in which the title of the action and its number have been entered.

107.   Thus the rule shall have the effect subject to the provisions of the Act, and these rules in particular, to any enactment which provides for the manner in which documents may be served on bodies corporate.

108.   Generally the desired mode of service of documents is personal service. There are a number of exceptions to personal service and these include:

(1)   Where instead of being served personally, the originating summons is served by post rule under Order 10 Rule 1(2)(a) of the RSC.

(2)   Where a defendant's legal practitioner endorses on the writ or other originating process that he/she accepts service on behalf of the defendant Rule 1(4).

(3)   Where a defendant acknowledges service, Rule 1(5).

(4)   Where an order for substituted service is made under Order 65 Rule 4.

(5)   Where in an action of contract, the contract specifies the manner on place of service Rule 3.

(6)   Where in action for an order for possession of land, the Court authorizes service to be effected by affixing on copy of the writ to some conspicuous part of the land Rule 4.

(7)   Where service is effected in a foreign country in accordance with the law of that country (Order 11 Rule 5(3)).

(8)   Service of originating summons in summary proceedings for possession of land (Order 113 Rule 4).

109.   In *Kenneth Allision Ltd v. A.E. Limehouse & Co* [1992] 2AC 105, it was held that the various provisions of the rules of the Supreme Court are not mandatory. Service may be made in accordance with the agreement of the parties. The parties are not restricted by Order 10 Rule 3 of the RSC.

110.   In *Mwase v. Pamela Brooks,* Civil Cause No. 1866 of 1994, the summons was sent to the last known address when the defendant had left the jurisdiction. The Court held that judgment entered in default of appearance was invalid for want of proper service.

§3.   SERVICE OUTSIDE THE JURISDICTION

111.   The common law rules relating to the competence of the High Court to entertain proceedings brought in person are procedural in character. Anyone may invoke the jurisdiction of the High Court or become subject to it, provided only that the defendant has been served with a writ of summons or its equivalent.

112.   The rule is that the defendant must be served regardless of his/her domicile, and a fleeting presence will suffice for service, as per *Colt Industries v. Sarlie* [1966] 1AllER 673. The Common Law Procedure Act of 1852 gave the Court discretionary power to grant the plaintiff leave to serve a writ outside the jurisdiction, in special circumstances.

113.   The principal cases in which service outside the jurisdiction may be made are outlined in Order 11 Rule 1 of the RSC, which include where the contract is governed by English law, where property is domiciled in the jurisdiction or where one of the parties is based in the jurisdiction, etc. Provided that the writ does not contain a claim mentioned in Order 75 Rule 2(1) and is not a writ to which paragraph 2 of this rule applies, service of the writ outside the jurisdiction is permissible with the leave of the Court in an action begun by writ.

(a)   Relief sought is against a person domiciled within the jurisdiction.
(b)   An injunction is sought ordering the defendant to do or refrain from doing anything within the jurisdiction and a person out of the jurisdiction is a necessary or proper party thereto.
(c)   The claim is brought to enforce, rescind, dissolve, annul or otherwise affect a contract or to recover damages or obtain other relief in respect of the breach of a contract, being (in either case) a contract which:
   (i)   was made within the jurisdiction;
   (ii)   was made by or though an agent trading or residing within the jurisdiction on behalf of the principal trading or residing out of the jurisdiction; or
   (iii)   by its terms or by implication governed by English law;[1]
   (iv)   contains a term to the effect that the High Court shall have jurisdiction to hear and determine any action in respect of the contract.

(d)   The claim is brought in respect of a breach committed within the jurisdiction of a contract made within or outside the jurisdiction and irrespective of whether it be the case that the breach was preceded or accompanied by a breach committed out of the jurisdiction that rendered impossible the performance of so much of the contract as ought to have been performed within the jurisdiction.

(e)   The claim is founded on a tort and the damage was sustained from an act committed, within the jurisdiction.

(f)   The whole subject matter of the action is land situated within the jurisdiction (with or without rent or profits) or the perpetuation of testimony relating to the land so situate.

(g)   The claim is brought to construe, rectify, set aside or enforce an act, deed, will, contract, obligation or liability affecting land situated within the jurisdiction.

(h)   The claim is made for a debt secured on immovable property or is made to assert, declare or determine proprietary or possessory rights or rights of security, in or over moveable property or to obtain authority to dispose of moveable property situated within the jurisdiction.

(i)   The claim is brought to execute the trusts or written instrument by trusts that ought to be executed according to English law and of which the person to be served with the writ is a trustee, or for any relief or remedy which might be obtained in any such action.

(j)   The claim is made for the administration of the estate of a person who died, domiciled within the jurisdiction, or for any relief or remedy which might be obtained in any such action.

(k)   The claim is brought to enforce any judgment or arbitral award.

(l)   The claim is brought for money had and received for an account or other relief against the defendant as constructive trustee, and the defendants' alleged liability arises out of acts committed, whether by him/her or otherwise, within the jurisdiction.

---

1.   English law is substituted by Malawian Law in this context.

114.   The nature of claims covered under Order 11 is wide. However, there is a need to show a connection with the jurisdiction of Malawi in order to have an order made under the rule.

115.   Order 11 Rule 2 provides that service of a writ on a defendant out of jurisdiction is permissible with the leave of the Court. The Court may direct the time within which the writ must be acknowledged under Order 11 Rule 2(3).

116.   Applications for leave are made ex parte before the Registrar. The application must be supported by a clear and frank affidavit setting out the relevant facts. In obtaining leave, full disclosure is necessary.

§4.   FORUM NON CONVENIENS

117.   The need to show that the case is a proper one for service outside the jurisdiction also manifests itself in the Court's discretion to refuse leave on the basis of forum non conveniens. The leading case is *Spilida Malitinie Corp v. Consuliea Ltd* [1987] AC 460. The plaintiff ship owner sought leave to serve an English writ on Canadian sulphur exporters, claiming damages in respect of severe corrosion to the hold of their ship, the Spilida, allegedly caused by a cargo of wet sulphur. An almost identical action just came up for trial before the Cambridgeshire Court, in England. The defendants in both cases were the same and the plaintiffs in both cases were the same insurer through subrogation; the insurer, rather than the nominal plaintiffs, had a real interest in bringing the proceedings. Cambridgeshire was in the nature of a test case. Lord Goff of Cheverly laid down the general principle that the Court has to identify the form in which the case can be tried in the interests of all the parties and for the ends of justice. The burden of proof rests on the plaintiff to show that England is the most appropriate place for the trial of the action. Factors to be considered by the Court when deciding whether to exercise its discretion to grant leave include the residence or place of business of the defendant and the ground invoked by the plaintiff.

118. The Court granted leave on the basis of *The Spilida(supra)*.

119. The Courts have the discretion to prevent unsuitable actions proceeding since *The Abidin Daver* (1984) AC 398, HC. The Court has to consider whether there is an alternative forum for the trial of the action. In *Macshemon v. Rockware Glass Ltd* [1978] AC 795, HL, a Scots employee sued his employer, which was registered in England, in respect of an accident in Scotland. All the witnesses lived in Scotland and clearly Scotland was the natural forum. Recently the Court held in *Roscoe v. Roscoe*[1] that the High Court of Malawi had no jurisdiction to hear divorce proceedings between parties domiciled in Zambia.

   1. Matrimonial cause no.7 of 2005.

§5. SERVICE OF DOCUMENTS: ORDER 65

120. Order 65 RSC also provides for service of documents like Order 10 RSC.

121. Order 65 Rule 1(5) provides that any document which by virtue of these rules is required to be served on any person need not be served personally unless the document is one which, by an express provision of these rules or by order of the Court, is required to be so served. Order 65 Rule 1(1) shall not affect the power of the Court to dispense with personal service requirements.

122. Order 65 Rule 1 provides that personal service is effected by leaving a copy of the document with the person to be served.

123. There are two types of documents which require personal service

(1)   any documents to be served on persons other than plaintiffs or other parties to the cause who have acknowledged service of the writ or other originating process, order obedience which may be enforced by committal or sequestration. Other documents however need not be served personally but can be served in any of the modes mentioned in rule 5. Personal service is a requisite for the following documents:

— Writ of summons.
— Amended writ of summons without leave and before service unless the Court directs otherwise.
— Writ of summons for service outside the jurisdiction.
— Third party notice to a person not a party to the action.
— Defence and counterclaim to a person not a party to the action.
— Originating summons.
— Originating notice of motion.
— Originating petition.
— Summons to attend the registrar in Chambers.
— Summons for leave to enforce a representative judgment.
— Judgment against a non-party.
— Order to carry on proceedings, to be served on a person who is not already a party thereto.
— Summons for leave to issue execution against a partner under judgment against a firm Order 81 Rule 5(4).
— an order to do an act (unless it is an order for discovery or inspection of documents) Order 24 Rule 16 or for interrogatories Order 26 Rule 6 if it is intended to enforce by committal Order 45 Rule 7.
— Notice of motion for committal in cases to which Order 52 Rule 3(3) applies unless the Court dispenses with such service.
— Notice of motion to issue a writ of sequestration Order 46 Rule 5(2) unless the Court dispenses with service under Order 46 Rule 5(3).
— Notice of Motion for committal.
— Writ of habeas corpus *ad subjiciendum*, if personal service is permissible.
— Writ of subpoena Order 38 Rule 17.
— A *garnishee nisi* (when being served on the garnishee) Order 49 Rule 3(1)(a).
— An order for examination of a judgment debtor Order 48 Rule 1.
— A notice of registration of a foreign judgment may be served either personally or by sending it to the judgment debtor at his/her usual or last known address Order 71 Rule 7.

§6. Manner of effecting personal service

124.   To effect personal service, the clerk or process server entrusted with the task should first satisfy him/herself that he/she has found the correct person. He/she should then hand it over or leave it with the person to be served with a copy of the writ. If the person served will not take the copy he/she should tell him/her what it contains and leave it as nearly in his/her possession or control as he/she can.

125.   If the defendant refuses to take the copy it is not necessary to leave it in his/her actual corporeal possession and it is sufficient to inform him/her of its nature and throw it down in his/her presence as per Patterson J in *Thomas v. Pheney* (1832) 1 Dowl. 441; yet this must be done in such circumstances as to bring the case within the above rule. Under Order 65 Rule 2 no process can be served on a Sunday. However a writ may be served on any day or time of the day.

126.   It was formerly held that service of process in the sight of the Court was contempt of Court. In *R v. Jones exp Mc Vittie* [1931] 1KB 664 it was held that such service might be a contempt. In *Poole v. Gould* (1856) 1 H&N 99 the Court refused to set aside personal service of a writ of summons on the defendant, effected in the Court where he/she was attending as a witness in another action, on the ground that every opportunity ought to be afforded to persons to serve debtors with writs.

§7. PERSONAL SERVICE ON A DEFENDANT IN PRISON

127.   To effect personal service on a prisoner, the plaintiff should apply to the governor of the prison where the defendant is confirmed and he/she will afford facilities for service.

128.   Order 65 Rule 3(1) provides that personal service of a document on a body cooperate may, in cases for which provision is not otherwise made by any enactment, be effected by serving it in accordance with Rule 2, on the major, chairman or president of the assembly or the town clerk, secretary, treasurer or other similar officer thereof. Order 65 Rule 3(1) provides that service may be made by the usual or last known address.

§8. SUBSTITUTED SERVICE (RULE 4)

129.   If personal service is impracticable for any reason, the Court may make an order for substituted service of that document. An application for substituted service may be made by summons supported by an affidavit stating the facts on which the application is founded.

130.   Substituted service of a document in relation to which the order relates is effected by taking such steps as the Court may prescribe to having the document to the notice of the person to be served.

131.   An order for substituted service may be through service on an agent or service by way of advertisement. The applicable date of service is the date of the advertisement or the service on the agent.

§9. ORDINARY SERVICE

132. Order 65 Rule 5 provides for ordinary service by way of personal service at the proper address of the person to be served, by post, by fax and in such manner as the Court may direct.

133. Order 65 Rule 8 provides that the person serving the document must swear an affidavit of service stating by whom the document was served, the day of the week on which it was served, where it was served and how.

134. Section 2 of the General Interpretation Act[1] has defined documents as to include any matter written, imposed or inscribed upon any substance by means of letters, figures or marks or by more than one of those means, which is intended to be used or may be used for purposes of according that matter. The definition covers a wider range of things.

  1. Cap 1:01 of the Laws of Malawi.

§10. SERVICE OF PROCESS AND EXECUTION OF JUDGMENTS ACT CAP 4:04 OF LAWS OF MALAWI

135. The Acts provides for service of process between Malawi, Zambia and Zimbabwe. This Act was made following creation of the Federation of Rhodesia and Nyasaland.[1] The application of the Act observed is more in breach than in compliance. The Act permits service and enforcement of judgments across the borders of the three countries. Currently, very little regard is made to this Act by legal practitioners since the dissolution of the Federation in 1963. The three countries apply different procedural rules with regard to service.

  1. The Federation was dissolved in 1963 and it led to independence of Malawi and Zambia in 1964 and later Zimbabwe in 1981.

§11. IMMUNITIES AND PRIVILEGES ACT, CAP 16:01[1]

136. Section 14 regulates the service of process and default judgments on diplomatic missions and foreign governments. It provides:

(1) Any process or other document required to be served for instituting proceedings against a State shall be served by being transmitted through the Ministry of External Affairs to the Ministry of Foreign Affairs of that State and service shall be deemed to have been effected when the process or other document is received at the State's Ministry.
(2) Any time for entering an appearance (whether prescribed by rules of court or otherwise) shall begin to run two months after the date on which the process or document is received at the State's Ministry.

(3) A State which appears in proceedings cannot thereafter raise any objection on the ground that subsection (1) has not been complied with in the case of those proceedings.

(4) No judgment in default of appearance shall be given against a State except on proof that subsection (1) has been complied with and that the time for entering an appearance as extended by subsection (2) has expired.

(5) A copy of any judgment given against a State in default of appearance shall be transmitted through the Ministry of External Affairs to the Ministry of Foreign Affairs of that State and any time for applying to have the judgment set aside (whether prescribed by rules of court or otherwise) shall begin to run two months after the date on which the copy of the judgment is received at that State's Ministry.

(6) Subsection (1) does not prevent the service of a process or other document in any manner to which the State has agreed and subsections (2) and (4) do not apply where service is effected in any such manner.

(7) This section shall not be construed as applying to proceedings against a State by way of counter-claim or to an action in rem, and subsection (1) shall not be construed as affecting any rules of court whereby leave is required for the service of process outside the jurisdiction.

    1. Laws of Malawi.

§12. COMPANIES ACT, CAP 46:03

   137. Section 137 of the Companies Act provides that:

(1) A document may be served on a company by leaving it at the registered office of the company or sending it by post to the registered postal address of the company.

(2) Any document to be served by post on a company shall be posted in such time as to admit of its being delivered in due course of delivery within the time, if any, prescribed for the service thereof; and in proving service it shall be sufficient to prove that a letter containing such document was properly addressed, prepared and posted, whether or not by registered post.

(3) If a company has no registered office or no registered postal address, service upon any director or the secretary of the company or, if the company has no director or secretary or if no director or secretary can be traced in Malawi, upon any member of the company, shall be deemed good and effectual service upon such company.

(4) If it shall be proved that any document was in fact received by any director or the secretary of a company such documents shall be deemed to have been served on the company notwithstanding that service may not have been effected in accordance with the foregoing subsections.

(5) Nothing in this section shall derogate from any provision in this Act relating to the service of any document, or from the power of any court to direct how

service shall be effected of any document relating to legal proceedings before that court.

(6)   Where a document is sent by post service shall be deemed to be effected by properly addressing, prepaying and posting a letter containing the document and to have been effected at the expiration of seven days or, if it is sent to an address outside Malawi, fourteen days after the letter containing the same is posted. The letter need not be dispatched by registered post but where it is sent to an address outside Malawi it shall be dispatched by airmail.

138.   In *Cheeseborough Ponds Mw Ltd v. Gala Estates Ltd,* Civil Cause No. 601 of 1988, the Deputy Registrar emphasized the need to comply with section 137 in serving process at the registered address.

139.   Service of documents is important so that the defendant is given an opportunity to present his/her side of the case in Court. The defendant must exercise his/her fundamental right to be heard that is, *audi alteram partem.* However if all efforts have been made to make a defendant aware of the proceedings and the defendant does not appear at the hearing, the Court will proceed with the hearing in his/her absence. The defendant must be accorded an opportunity to be heard and it is up to him/her to seize the same.

140.   However in the event that the defendant was not served, the proceedings will be set aside; hence there is need for great care to ensure that the parties have been properly served with all documents and processes in order to avoid wasting the Court's time and costs.

Chapter 6. Parties, Joinder and Misjoinder of Actions and Parties

§1. PARTIES AND CAUSES OF ACTION

141. Parties are regulated under Orders 15,80, 81 and 83 of the RSC. The specific parties include several defendants and several plaintiffs several causes of action, partners and minors.

§2. JOINDER OF CAUSES OF ACTION

142. Order 15 Rule 1 provides:

(1) Subject to rule 5(1) a plaintiff may in one action claim relief against the defendant in respect of more than one cause of action:-
   (a) if the plaintiff claims, and the defendant is liable or is alleged to be liable, in the same capacity in respect of all the causes of action; or
   (b) if the plaintiff claims or the defendant is alleged to be liable in the capacity of executor or administrator of an estate in respect of one or more causes of action and in his personal capacity but with reference to the same estate in respect of all others, or
   (c) with leave of the court.
(2) An application for leave under this rule must be made ex parte by affidavit before issue of writ of originating summons, as the case may be, and the affidavit must state the grounds of the application.

143. Under this rule claims for defamation, malicious prosecution and false imprisonment have been categorized together. However the statement of claim needs to state the facts in support of each case separately. The cause of action has been defined to comprise every fact which it would be necessary for the plaintiff to prove, if traversed; to support the judgment of the Court see *Read v. Brown* (1888) 2 QBD 128, as per Lord Esher M.R. at 131. If the plaintiff alleges facts which if not traversed would entitle him/her to recover then he/she makes out a cause of action as per Lord Esher in *Cotarn v. College* [1897] 1 QB702 at 707. In *Letang v. Cooper* [1965] 1QB 232 at 242 it was defined as simply a factual situation the existence of which entitles a person to obtain from the Court a remedy against another person, as per Diplock LJ.

144. However, it is clear under Order 15 Rule 1 that the same person cannot be plaintiff and defendant in the same summons, unless there is a counterclaim against the plaintiff, then the defendant can be made plaintiff in the same action and the counterclaim is taken as an independent action.

145. Claims by executor or administrator may be made together, for example, loss of dependency and loss of expectation of life. A person may require a grant of probate or letters of administration to prove a claim for loss or expectation of life, and you may not require the same to prove a claim for loss of dependency see *Mbaisa v. Ismael Brothers,*[1] *Ingolosi v. Mohamed.*[2]

1. 6 ALR Mal 321.
2. 6 ALR Mal 335 This position was reaffirmed in *Dalitso Banje v. Mr Issa Civil Cause* no. 265 of 1997 where it was held by Kumange J that a claim for recession of contract would not have been made in the absence of letters of administration.

146.   Leave of the Court may be granted in exceptional circumstances to join various causes of action. However such joinder may be subject to objections and delay.

147.   Where a defendant is of the view that the causes of action were improperly joined, the defendant may give notice of intention to defend, and apply to set aside the writ under Order 12 of Rule 8 of RSC. Subject to an order for costs, the Court may grant leave retrospectively.

§3. COUNTERCLAIM AGAINST THE PLAINTIFFS

148.   Subject to Order 15 Rule 5(2), a defendant in any action, who alleges that he/she has a claim or is entitled to any relief or remedy against a plaintiff in the action in respect of any matter, wherever and however arising, may, instead of bringing a separate action, make a counterclaim in respect of the matter, and where he/she does so, he/she must add the counterclaim to his/her defence.

149.   Rule 1 shall apply in relation to a counterclaim as if the counterclaim were a separate action and as if the person making the counterclaim were the plaintiff and the person against whom it is made were a defendant.

150.   A counterclaim may be proceeded with, notwithstanding that the judgment is given for the plaintiff in the action or that action is stayed.

151.   Where a defendant establishes a counterclaim against the claim of the plaintiff and there is a balance in favour of one of the parties, the balance, so however, that his/her provision shall not be taken as affecting the Court's discretion with respect to costs.

152.   A counterclaim is generally taken as an independent action. A counterclaim may be made for either liquidated or un-liquidated damages and may exceed the amount of the plaintiff's claim. It is however convenient that the actions be tried together with the plaintiff's claim. The Limitation Act[1] applies to a counterclaim. A counterclaim must be of such a nature that the Court would have jurisdiction to entertain it as separate case, as per *Bow Mclachlan & Co. Ltd v. Ship Canon* [1909] AC 997. It is generally treated as an independent action in terms of Bowen LJ in *Amon v. Bobbett* 22QBD 543 at 548.

1. Cap 6:01 of the Laws of Malawi.

153. Counterclaim to counterclaim may be permitted even though the plaintiffs counterclaim may be more than mere protection against the defendant's counterclaim and even though the cause of action on which it is founded arose after the issue of the writ. *Joke v. Andrews* (1882) 8 QBD 428 *Renton Gibbo & Co Ltd v. Neville & Co* [1900] 2QB 181 CA.

154. A defendant claiming against a third party may counterclaim against the counterclaim made by a third party see *The Normar* [1968] 1 AllER 753.

155. Counterclaim against additional parties under Order 15 Rule 3(1) where the defendant to an action makes a counterclaim against the plaintiff which alleges that any other person (whether or not a party to the action) is liable to him/her along with the plaintiff. In counterclaim or claims against such other person or any relief relating or connected with the original subject matter of the action, then, subject to Rule 5(7) he/she may join that other person as a party against whom the counterclaim is made.

156. However, a counterclaim must be made in the time within which the defendant should have served his/her defence in terms of Order 18 Rule 2.

§4. JOINDER OF PARTIES

157. Under Order 15 Rule 4 of the RSC, two or more persons may be joined together in one action as plaintiffs or as defendants, with the leave of the Court, where:

(a) separate actions were brought by or, as the case may be, some question of law or fact which would arise in all the actions; and
(b) all rights to relief claimed in the action (whether they are joint or several) are in respect of or arise out of the same transaction or a series of transactions.

158. The rule requires that identical investigations be performed together, as established in *Market & Co v. Knight Steamship* [1910] 2KB 1021. The relief may also arise out of the same transaction or the same set of circumstances, see *Stroud v. Lawson* [1898] 2QB54.

§5. SEPARATE TRIALS

159. Under Order 15 Rule 5(1) the Court may order separate trials or make such other order as it deems fit if it appears that the joinder of causes of action or of the parties as the case may be, may embarrass or delay the trial, or is otherwise inconvenient.

160. Under Order 15 Rule 5(2) a party may apply for a separate trial for any reason of the counterclaim. The Court may order that the counterclaim be struck out or that the counterclaim be tried separately upon application, or indeed make any other order as may be deemed expedient.

161.   The courts have supervisory control over joinder or misjoinder of the parties or joinder of causes of action. The Court has power to prevent embarrassing joinders or misjoinders.

§6. MISJOINDER OR NON-JOINDER OF THE PARTIES

162.   Under Order 15 Rule 6(1) no cause or matter shall be defeated by reason of the misjoinder or non-joinder of any party, and the Court may, for any cause or matter, determine the issues or questions in dispute so far as they affect the rights and interests of the persons who are parties to the cause or matter.

163.   The Court has wide powers under Order 15 Rule 6(2):

(a)   to order any party who has been improperly or unnecessarily made a party or who has for any reason ceased to be a proper or necessary party to cease to be a party.
(b)   order any of the following persons to be added as a party, namely
  (i)   any person who ought to have been joined as a party or whose presence before the court is necessary to ensure that all the matters in dispute in the cause or matter may be effectually or completely determined and adjudicated upon; or
  (ii)   any person between whom and any party to the cause or matter there may exist a question or issue arising out of or relating to or connected with any relief or remedy claimed in the cause or matter which in the opinion of the court it would be just and convenient to determine as between him and that party as well as between the parties to the cause or matter.

164.   Order 15 Rule 6(3) provides that an application for an order under paragraph (2) that a non-party be added as a party must, except with leave of the Court, be supported by an affidavit showing his/her interest in the matters in dispute or matter to which, in the opinion of the Court, it would be just and convenient to determine, as between him/her and any party to the cause or matter.

165.   Under Order15 Rule 6(4) no person shall be added as a plaintiff without his/her consent or as may be authorized.

166.   Under Order 15 Rule 6(5) there can be no addition or substitution of parties after the expiry of the period of limitation.

§7. Intervention by Person not Party

167. Generally in common law, a plaintiff who conceives that he/she has a cause of action against a defendant is entitled to pursue his/her remedy against that defendant alone. he/she cannot be compelled to proceed against other persons whom he/she has no desire to sue as established under *Dollfus Mieg etc v. Bank of England* [1951] Ch 33 and *The State v. Speaker of National Assembly ex parte Yunus Mussa and 41 others.*[1]

1. Miscellaneous civil cause no. 61 of 2007 where Singini J. declined an application by The United Democratic Front and Dr Nga Ntafu to join judicial review proceedings. Dr Ntafu Member of Parliament and United Democratic Front a political party in opposition in parliament sought to join proceedings against the Speaker by some members of parliament against whom the speaker had issued petitions on whether they had crossed the floor in parliament.

168. A person who is not a party may be added as a defendant against the wishes of the plaintiff, either on application by the defendant, on his/her own intention or, in rare cases, by the Court, of its own motion. The jurisdiction of the Court is entirely discretionary. The Court allows interventions by no parties in order to (a) prevent multiplicity of actions and enable the Court to determine disputes between all the parties to them in one action and (b) to prevent the same or substantially the same question or issues being tried twice with possibly different results.

169. In order to entitle a person to intervene and to be joined as a party, the rule requires that the would-be intervener should have some interest which is directly related to or connected with the subject matter of the action as established in *Sanders Lead Co. Inc v. Entires General Brokers Ltd* [1984] 1 WLR 587. CA.

170. Clearly what is contemplated is that at the time when an order for rejoinder is made under this provision, the question or issue arising out of or relating to or connected with the relief or remedy claimed in the cause already arises between the party seeking to be joined and one or the other of the existing parties as per Bridge L.J. in *Spelling Goldberg Productions v. BPC Publishing* [1981] RPC 280 at 281.

171. The Court has the power to correct mistakes in the names of plaintiffs or defendants. The Court may correct bona fide mistakes in the name of a plaintiff or a defendant and substitute with the name of the right party, where this can be done without causing the other party any prejudice or injury for which he/she cannot be compensated with the payment of costs. The power to amend the action is also available under Order 20 Rule 13 RSC as per *Bazuka & Co. v. M.B. Phekani & Sons* 10 MLR 332, *Khembo CBS Industries v. Roberts Construction (Mw) Ltd* 8 MLR 333 and *African Businessmen Association (Mw) v. Muwamba Banda and Constantini and Company Ltd* 10MLR 221.

§8. PROCEEDINGS AGAINST DECEASED ESTATES

172. Under Order 15 Rule 6A of the RSC, where any person against whom an action would have existed has died but the cause of action survives, the action may, if no grant of probate or administrator has been made, be brought against the estate of the deceased.[1] The action is generally treated to have been commenced by the estate of a deceased person. Under Order 15 Rule 6A(3) it does not matter whether a grant has been made or not in order to proceed in an action against a dead man. The Court may allow amendments on application by any party at any stage. Under Order 15 Rule 6A(7) of the rule, any order or judgment shall bind the estate in the same way as it would have been made and a personal representative of the deceased had been a party to the proceedings.

    1. *Dalitso Banje v. Issa (supra).*

§9. CHANGE OF PARTIES BY REASON OF DEATH

173. Under Order 15 Rule 7(1) where a party dies or becomes bankrupt but the cause of action survives, the action shall not abate by reason of the death or bankruptcy. The Court may make an order for substitution of the party and the action shall proceed notwithstanding the bankruptcy or death. The application shall be under Order 15 Rule 9 (1). Personal representatives of a deceased person may apply for an order that unless the action proceeds within some specified time, it shall be dismissed.

§10. SPECIFIC PARTIES

174. Special parties refers to individuals, next friends and guardians ad litem, partnerships, representatives and relators.

§11. INDIVIDUALS

175. Individuals should give their full names in all court documents. Initials should be rarely used. A litigant who changes a name for example, upon marriage, must file a notice of change at the court office and serve it on the other parties.

§12. NEXT FRIENDS AND GUARDIANS AD LITEM

176. A person under disability must sue by a next friend and be sued by a guardian ad litem in terms of Order 80 Rule 2 of the RSC. A minor's next friend is normally a relative with no interest in the litigation adverse to that of the minor. A mental patient's next friend or guardian is usually a receiver appointed under the Mental Health and Treatment Act.[1] Where a person under disability has no next friend or guardian ad litem, an application can be made for a suitable person to be appointed by the Court. A next friend must act through a legal practitioner and must file a written consent to so act. All services of process must be served on the next friend or guardian ad litem under Order 80 Rule 16.

1. Cap 34:02 of the Laws of Malawi.

177.   In case of settlement of monetary claims, the Court must approve all settlements involving minors in order to give a valid discharge for the money to be paid and ensure that there can be no question of unfairness to the person under disability, in terms of Order 80 Rule 11 RSC. The approval is sought by issue of an expedited originating summons setting out the claim and seeking the Court's approval of the settlement and such other orders to give necessary effect to it. This also applies where no proceedings have been commenced if the settlement is to be valid. Approval is sought by way of summons. The Court may order payment into court in order to prevent the funds being used for the general benefit of the minor's family.

§13. PARTNERSHIPS

178.   The liability of partners is generally joint and several.[1] They may be sued either in their individual names or in the name of the firm, adding the words 'a firm' in the heading, as set out under Order 81 Rule 1 RSC.

1. Section 10, Partnership Act cap 46:03 of the Laws of Malawi.

179.   The process may be served on the partnership and may be effected on any one of the partners, any person having control or management of the firm's principal place of business or by sending the writ to the firm's principal place of business in terms of Order 81 Rule 3 RSC. However, where the partnership has been dissolved, all partners must be served individually.

180.   A partner served with a writ in the name of the firm must acknowledge service in his/her name. The proceedings continue in the name of the firm. A person served as a partner who denies being one at the relevant time should state that denial when acknowledging. The acknowledgement may then be set aside on the ground that the partner was liable at such relevant time or alternatively, the defendant may apply to set aside service or plead the denial in the defence under Order 81 Rule 4 RSC. Under Order 81 Rule 2, parties sued by or suing partnerships may serve notice requiring disclosure of names and addresses of partners.

181.   Compliance may be sought by application to court. Judgments may be enforced against partnership property or against the property of the person who is admitted to be a partner in the action. Enforcement against other persons is only by leave of the Court.

§14. REPRESENTATIVE PROCEEDINGS

182.   Order 15 Rule 12(1) provides:

Where numerous persons have the same interest in any proceedings, not being such proceedings as are mentioned in rule 13, the proceedings may begin, and unless the Court otherwise orders, continued by or against anyone of them as representing all or as representing all except one of them.

183.   According to *Duke of Bedford v. Ellis* [1901] AC1, persons will have the same interests if they have a common interest or they have a common grievance and the relief sought is, in its nature, beneficial to all whom the plaintiff proposes to represent. A judgment obtained in representative proceedings binds everyone in the class represented but can only be enforced with the leave of the court.

§15. RELATOR ACTIONS

184.   Before the name of any person is used in any action as a relator, that person must give a written authorization so to use his/her name to a legal practitioner and the authorization must be filed in the court office or if the writ is to issue out of a district registry, in such registry.

185.   A relator action is one in which a person or body claiming to be entitled to restrain interference with a public right or to abate a public nuisance or to compel the performance of a public duty, is bound to bring such action in the name of the Attorney General as a necessary party. The practice is to describe the plaintiff as 'The Attorney General at the relation of plaintiff (the relator)'. Where the relator has separate cause of action, arising out of the same facts, he/she may be added as co-plaintiff, as established under *Gouriet v. Union of Post Office Workers* [1978] AC 435.

186.   The jurisdiction of the Attorney General to decide in what cases it is proper for him/her to sue on behalf of relators is absolute and the Court has no power to review his/her decision, as per *London County Council v. Attorney General* [1902] AC 165 HC.

Chapter 7. Interpleaders

§1. Interpleader Proceedings

187. Interpleader proceedings may be used in two circumstances. In the first, a person holding money or goods or liable on a debt is, or expects to be, sued by two or more persons making adverse claims to the property in question. There are two types of interpleaders, viz., stakeholder's interpleader and sheriff's interpleader. The Court has the power to determine which of the interpleaders will be plaintiff or defendant. Interpleaders are regulated by Order 17 of the RSC and section 20 of the Sheriffs Act.[1] The object of the rule is to avoid the same action being tried twice with possibly different results, and to prevent multiplicity of actions between the parties.[2]

1. Cap 3:05 of the Laws of Malawi.
2. *Swift Transport Ltd v. Cooper Diesels Ltd* 2 ALR Mal 146 see also *Lesco v. Correia Construction Ltd* and Jones Stambuli Civil Cause no. 1194 of 2000.

§2. Sheriff's interpleader

188. Section 20 of the Sheriff's Act provides:

(1) If a person (hereinafter in this section referred to as the claimant) claims any movable property seized in execution under any process, or the proceeds or value thereof, he shall first give notice in writing thereof to the Sheriff in such form, if any, as may be prescribed. The Sheriff shall thereupon serve copies of such notice in the manner prescribed for the service of any document of the court out of which the process issued upon the execution creditor and upon any other person he considers to be interested in the property.

(2) The Sheriff shall hold the property claimed for 14 days from the date upon which the last person was served with a copy of the claim under subsection (1) and if such claim is not disputed by any of the persons upon whom copies of the claimant's notice have been so served within such 14 days the Sheriff may deliver the property in question to the claimant.

(3) If the claimant's claim is disputed, the person disputing it shall give notice in writing in such form, if any, as may be prescribed to the Sheriff, who shall forthwith apply to the court from which the process was issued and such court shall issue a summons calling before the court the party at whose instance the process issued and the claimant.

(4) Upon the issue of the summons, any action brought in any court in respect of the claim or of any damage arising out of the execution of the warrant shall be stayed.

(5) On the hearing of the summons, the court shall adjudicate upon the claim, and shall also adjudicate between the parties or either of them and the Sheriff upon any claim to damages arising or capable of arising out of the

execution of the warrant by the Sheriff, and shall make such order in respect
of any such claim and the costs of the proceedings as it thinks fit.

§3. STAKEHOLDER'S INTERPLEADER

189.   If proceedings have not been commenced against the person in possession
of the property, the application is made by expedited originating summons, and if
the proceedings are already pending, the application is made by ordinary interlocutory summons. The summons must be served on the existing plaintiff if made in
pending proceedings, and on all claimants to the property. This procedure is provided for under Order 17 Rule 3 of the RSC. The Court has the power, on the hearing date, to order that the claimant be made defendant in proceedings, substitute the
parties, order that an issue be stated between the claimants with direction as to
which is plaintiff or defendant, determine the issues summarily or make such other
order as may be just.

Chapter 8. Third-Party Actions

§1. THIRD PARTY PROCEEDINGS

190. Under Order 16 RSC, a defendant to an existing action is permitted within certain limits to bring a claim against a non-party by issuing a third party notice. The procedure allows a defendant to pass on the action to the third party. A defendant with a claim against a non-party has the alternative option of commencing separate proceedings.

191. In order to minimize costs, to avoid multiplicity of actions and to avoid the danger of inconsistent judgments, third party proceedings are more convenient.

§2. THIRD PARTY NOTICE

192. Under Order 16 Rule 1, where in any action, a defendant has given notice of intention to defend:

(a) claims against a person not already a party to the action for any contribution or indemnity; or
(b) claims against such a person seeking any relief or remedy relating or connected with the original subject matter of the action and substantially the same as some relief or remedy claimed by the plaintiff; or
(c) requires that any question or issue relating to or connected with the original subject matter of the action should be determined not only as between either or with or both of them and a person not already a party to the issue, a notice (third party notice) containing a statement of the nature of the claim made against him/her and, as the case may be, of either nature and grounds of the claim made by him/her or the question or issue required to be determined.

193. Under Order 16 Rule 1(2) a defendant may not issue a third party notice without the leave of the Court unless the action was begun by writ and he/she issues the notice before serving his/her defence on the plaintiff. After service, the third party has the same rights of defending the action as a defendant.

§3. SCOPE OF THIRD PARTY PROCEEDINGS

194. Third party proceedings cover issues of contributory indemnity and related relief.

§4. CONTRIBUTION

195. A right to contribution arises where there are joint tortfeasors, such as where there is more than one driver responsible for a road accident, the Court needs to assess the relative degrees of blame attending to each of the drivers. Contribution is bottomed and fixed on general principles of practice and does not spring from contract, through contract may qualify it, as per *Dering v. Winchelsea* (1787) 1 Cox 318. Liability of joint tortfeasors is governed by section 11 of the Statute Law (Miscellaneous Provisions) Act.[1]

1. Cap 5:01 of the Laws of Malawi.

§5. INDEMNITY

196.   Whereas a right to contribute has the effect of sharing the responsibility to the plaintiff, the effect of aim indemnity is that the defendant can recover the entirety of his/her liability to the plaintiff from a third party. Entitlement to an indemnity may arise by contract, under statute or by virtue of the relationship between the parties.

197.   A common case of indemnities arising by contract is the contract of insurance. A defendant sued in respect of an insured risk could issue a third party notice claiming an indemnity against the answer, although this will be unnecessary if the insurers may be sued directly under section 148 of the Road Traffic Act.[1]

1. Cap 69:01 of the Laws of Malawi.

198.   Indemnities arising by virtue of the relationship between the parties depend on the substantive law.

199.   An application for leave to issue a third party notice may be made ex parte but the Court may direct a summons for leave to be issued.

200.   Under Order 16 Rule 2(2) RSC, an application for leave to issue a third party notice must be supported by an affidavit stating the nature of the claim made by the plaintiff in the action, the stage at which the proceedings have reached the nature of the claim made by the applicant or particulars of the question or issue required to be determined as the case may be, and the facts on which the proposed third party notice is based and the name and address of the person against whom the third party notice is to be issued.

§6. ISSUE SERVICE AND ACKNOWLEDGEMENT OF THIRD PARTY NOTICE

201.   Under Order 16 Rule 3 the order granting leave to issue a third party notice may contain directions as to the period within which the notice is to be issued. The notice may be served and acknowledged in the same way as the writ of summons may be served and acknowledged, as the case may be.

§7. THIRD PARTY NOTICE OF INTENTION TO DEFEND

202.   Under Order 16 Rule 4, if a third party gives notice of intention to defend, the defendant who issued a third party notice must, by summons to be served on all other parties to the Court, apply to the Court for directions. If no summons is served on the third party, the third party may, not earlier than seven days after giving notice of intention to defend by summons, apply to the Court for directions or for an order to set aside the third party notice.

203.   Upon the application for directions, the Court may, if liability is established, order such judgment as the case may require, order any claim or issue to be tried in such manner as the Court may direct and dismiss or terminate the proceedings on the third party notice.

204.   An order under Rule 4 may be rescinded or varied by the Court at any time.

§8. ENFORCEMENT OF JUDGMENT

205.   A defendant cannot enforce a judgment for the payment of a contribution or an indemnity from a third party without leave, until the plaintiff's claim has been satisfied, as per Order 16 Rule 7(2) RSC.

Chapter 9. Pleadings

§1. PLEADINGS

206. Pleadings include the statement of claim, defence, reply to defence and counterclaim, rejoinder, rebuttals and surrebuttals. These are the documents which outline a party's claim or defence, as the case may be. These documents are exchanged by the parties in the High Court. Pleadings have a number of functions and these include:

(a) To inform the other side of the case they will have to meet and ensure that they are not taken by surprise at all.
(b) To define the issues that need to be filed, so as to save costs at trial and to limit the ambit of discover and the evidence that needs to be prepared.
(c) To provide the trial judge with a precise statement of the contentions advanced by the parties. Pleadings are the first documents to be read by the trial judge hence they should be well drafted.[1]

> 1. *Yanu Yanu Bus Co Ltd v. Mbewe* 10 MLR 417, *Malawi Railways Ltd v. PTK Nyasulu* [1993] 16(1) MLR 394, *Finance Corporation of Malawi v. Malbro International MSCA* Civil Appeal No. 30 of 2000.

§2. FORM OF PLEADINGS

207. All pleadings must have proper headings including cause numbers and the nature of the pleading itself; that is, it must be stated whether it is statement of claim or defence.

208. Every pleading needs to contain the necessary particulars of any claim, defence or other matter intended to be advanced at the trial. (Order 18 Rule 12(1) RSC). It must, if necessary, be divided into numbered paragraphs, with each allegation being, as far as convenient, pleaded in chronological order and contained in a separate paragraph (Order 18 Rule 6(2) RSC). The allegations should be stated in a summary form and as briefly as the nature of the case permits. The parties are restricted to pleading facts which are material to the claim or defence advanced and must not plead evidence by which those facts are to be proved, as per Order 18 Rule 7(1) RSC. All pleadings must be signed by legal practitioners or the party in person in terms of Order 18 Rule 5(5) RSC.

209. Under Order 19 Rule 1, the plaintiff must serve a statement of claim on the defendant or defendants at the time of service of the writ or after service of the writ. The statement of claim may contain various causes of action arising out of the same facts claimed in the writ of summons in terms of Order 18 Rule 15(2) RSC; the primary function of the essential facts establishing the plaintiff's causes of action.

210. In personal injuries claims, the statement of claim must include the plaintiff's date of birth (*Practice Direction (Personal Injuries: Pleading)* [1974] 1 WLR 1427) and must be served with a medical report and a schedule of special damages. See Order 18 Rule 12 (1A).

211. Under Order 18 Rule 2 RSC, a defendant who gives notice of intention to defend must, unless the Court gives leave to the contrary, serve a defence before the expiration of fourteen days after the time limited for acknowledgment of service or after the statement of claim is served on him/her, whichever is later.

212. A plaintiff on whom a defendant serves defence must serve a reply on that defendant if it is needed. Order 18 Rule 3(1) RSC.

213. A plaintiff on whom a defendant serves a counterclaim must, if he/she intends to defend it, serve on that defendant a defence to counterclaim in terms of Order 18 Rule 3(2) RSC. A reply to defence and defence to counterclaim must be included in the same document and must be served within fourteen days after the service of defence.

214. Order 18 Rule 4 provides that there be no service of further pleadings after service of reply to defence without leave of the Court. These pleadings include rejoinder (by defendant), surrejoinder (by plaintiff), rebutter (be defendant), surrebutter (by plaintiff). The application to serve any of these pleadings has to be made to the Registrar by summons.

§3. FURTHER AND BETTER PARTICULARS

215. A party confronted with a pleading that does not give full particulars of the nature of claim or defence being advanced by the other side, such that there is a possibility of being surprised at trial, may serve a request for further and better particulars of the pleading in question. The request is headed in the same way as the pleading in the case. The party identifies a number of paragraphs being attacked, and sets out the passages that are said to give inadequate particulars. A request is then made for the specific further particulars sought. This is governed by Order 18 Rule 12 of the RSC. If the other party is not willing to comply with the request, then a request for the particulars may be made to the Registrar by summons.

216. In cases involving points of law or construction or which do not raise issues of fact, there may be trial without pleadings under Order 18 Rule 21 RSC.

§4. USE OF PLEADINGS AT TRIAL

217. The purpose of pleadings is to define the issues in the action, and the conduct of the trial is fixed by the pleadings. Evidence should only be provided on matters that have been pleaded and judgment will also be given only on matters that have been pleaded. *Lipkin Gorman v. Karpnale Ltd* [1989] 1WLR 1340. *Yanu Yanu Bus Co. Ltd v. Mbewe (supra) Malawi Railways Ltd v. P.T.K. Nyasulu (supra)*

218. The courts however do not permit parties to amend their pleadings in terms of Order 20 of the RSC.

Chapter 10. Affidavit Evidence

§1. AFFIDAVITS

219. Affidavits are sworn written statements by a witness in an action. Affidavits are drawn up by legal practitioners and their purpose is to place a witness' evidence before the Court in a convenient form.

220. In the High Court, affidavits are used in all proceedings commenced by originating summonses, originating motions or petitions and may also be used in interlocutory applications in writ actions. In most interlocutory applications there is need for an affidavit in support of application, for example, summons to set aside judgment, summons for an interlocutory injunction, summons for leave to serve outside the jurisdiction, summons for interim payment etc.

221. Under Order 41 Rule 1 RSC, every affidavit sworn in a cause or matter must be entitled in that cause or matter.

222. Order 41 Rule 1(4) requires that every affidavit must be expressed in the first person, stating the place of residence of the deponent, his/her occupation and whether he/she is employed by the party to the action. However deponents giving evidence in a professional capacity may, instead of giving the place of residence, state the address at which he/she works, the position he/she holds and the name of the firm or his/her employer, if any.

223. Under Order 41 Rule (4)5, every affidavit must be divided into paragraphs numbered consecutively, each paragraph being, as far as possible, confined to a distinct portion of the subject. Order 41 Rule 1(8) requires that every affidavit must be signed by the deponent, and the jurat must be completed and signed by the person before whom it is sworn. In Malawi, persons authorized to administer oaths are provided for under the Oaths, Affirmations and Declarations Act,[1] section 4. By virtue of section 4, an affidavit may be sworn before a legal practitioner, magistrate or other public officers acting as administrative officer or professional officer.

1. Cap 4:07 of the Laws of Malawi.

§2. EVIDENCE

224. Affidavits must only contain facts which the deponent can prove from his/her own knowledge, as per Order 41 Rule 5(1) RSC. In interlocutory proceedings, affidavits need to contain a statement of information or belief, provided the sources or grounds of such information or belief are stated, as established under Order 41 Rule 5(2) RSC. The rules allow admission of hearsay evidence and of the deponents' own opinion, but do not allow other forms of inadmissible evidence, such as the opinion of someone other than the deponent

(*Savings and Investment Bank Ltd v. Gasco Investment (Netherlands BV*) [1984] 1WLR271. Second-hand (hearsay) evidence may be also admitted under this rule.

225.   Affidavits must be pertinent to the issues and irrelevant matter or inadmissible material such as hearsay in affidavits used at trial may be struck out under Order 41 Rule 6 RSC.

§3. JURAT

226.   The deponent must sign, and the person before whom the affidavit is sworn must attest at the end of the affidavit. The jurat is statement of the person before whom and where the affidavit was sworn, and must be signed by that person.

§4. INTERLINEATIONS

227.   Any interlineations or alteration in an affidavit must be initialled by the person before whom the affidavit is sworn, in terms of Order 41 Rule 7 of the RSC.

§5. BINDING

228.   Affidavits need to be bound in book form. Exhibits to the affidavits must be bound separately. There is a prohibition in England on the use of a plastic strip binding for affidavits but in Malawi the rule is observed more in breach than in compliance.

§6. SPECIAL CASES

229.   An affidavit may exceptionally be sworn by two or more deponents under Order 41 Rule 2 RSC. If a deponent is blind or illiterate, the person before whom it is sworn must audibly read it to the deponent and certify that the deponent seemed to understand it, in terms of Order 41 Rule 3 of the RSC.

§7. EXHIBITS

230.   Any document or thing used in conjunction with an affidavit must be made an exhibit under Order 41 Rule 11 of the RSC. Letters and other documents may be exhibited, but not court documents. The prohibition on the use of court documents is that the court documents must prove themselves.

§8. FILING

231.   Under Order 41 Rule 9, affidavits used in documents must be filed at court, usually before the hearing.

§9. CHALLENGING VERACITY OF AFFIDAVITS

232.   Affidavits may be challenged in rare cases by filing a notice of intention to cross-examine deponents. This usually occurs in originating processes and not in interlocutory matters. The Court will rarely permit cross-examination of deponents in interlocutory matters. The Court will usually determine issues of relevance, admissibility and weight by looking at the affidavit itself.

Chapter 11. Interlocutory Matters

§1. INTERLOCUTORY PROCEDURE

233. In some cases it is desirable to obtain directions from the Court or orders of the Court before proceeding with the action, for example, leave to serve proceedings outside the jurisdiction, summons for substituted service etc. The directions are obtained by way of interlocutory applications. The nature of the applications varies widely and they can be made before the Registrar in chambers or before a judge in chambers. There may be uncontroversial applications and controversial ones. The applications may be made ex parte or inter parte. Most interlocutory applications need to be supported by affidavit evidence. Ex parte applications may be granted with proper reasons. The applications may be made by the party him/herself or his/her legal practitioner.

234. Applications before the Registrar or his/her Deputy or Assistant are made by way of summons supported by affidavit. The summons spells out clearly the relief sought. The Registrar allocates time for the hearing of the summons and normally there should be at least two clear days before the date of hearing, in terms of Order 32 Rule 3 of the RSC. In practice the courts will provide adequate time before the hearing of the summons. Respondents contesting the summons need to serve their affidavit in opposition before the return date. There are exceptions for the two-day rule for example:

(a) A summons asking only for the extension or abridgement of time (time summons) may be served before the return day (Order 32 Rule 3 RSC).

(b) A summons to assign a guardian ad litem must be served at least seven days before the return day (Order 80 Rule 6(5) RSC).

(c) A summons seeking summons judgment or an interim payment must be served 10 clear days before the return day (Order 14 Rule 2 and Order 29 Rule 10 RSC).

§2. ADJOURNMENT

235. Hearing of a summons may be adjourned from time to time under Order 32 Rule 4 (1)RSC. If the hearing is adjourned, generally, the party by whom the summons was taken out may restore it to the list upon two clear days' notice to all other parties on whom the summons was served under Order 32 Rule 4(2) RSC.

§3. PROCEEDING IN ABSENCE OF PARTY FAILING TO ATTEND

236. Where a party to a summons fails to attend the first or resumed hearing, the Court may proceed in his/her absence if, having regard to the nature of the application, it thinks expedient to do so, in terms of Order 32 Rule 5(1) RSC. The Court may have to satisfy itself with service of the summons. However under Order 32

Rule 5(3), where the Court proceeded in the absence of the other party, then any order made on the hearing that has not been perfected may still cause the Court to rehear the summons, if it is just to do so. The Court may also permit restoration of dismissed summons to the cause list.

237.   Under Order 32 Rule 26 RSC, any order made ex parte may be set aside ex parte. The Registrar has the power to direct that a summons be heard before a Judge in chambers and vice versa.

Chapter 12. Injunctions

§1. INJUNCTION

238. The courts may sometimes grant orders of injunction in order maintain the status quo; that is, prevent further damage from occurring. Injunction may also be granted in order to preserve property. There are six types of injunctions that can be granted in Malawi, viz.:

(1) Perpetual injunction that is, one which is granted at the end of the trial.
(2) Interlocutory injunction that is, one which may granted as a provisional order before trial.
(3) Interim injunction that is, granted ex parte until the return date of the motion. This will subsist between the ex parte and inter parte motion.
(4) Mandatory injunction that is, one which requires certain acts to be done.
(5) Prohibitive injunction that is, one restraining a person from doing certain actions.
(6) Quia timet injunction that is, an order to prevent an apprehended legal wrong when none has been committed at the date of the application.

239. In Malawi, injunctions can only be granted in the High Court by virtue of section 11 of the Courts Act. The applications are made before a Judge in Chambers.[1] The Registrar may only grant an injunction in a consent order under Order 32 Rule 11 RSC or the appointment of a receiver.

> 1. There has been lot of debate on the issuing of injunctions by the courts in Malawi. Numerous newspapers have reported on the issue. See M. Chilenga Dikastocracy in Malawi KAF Occasional Papers 2008.

§2. EX PARTE APPLICATIONS

240. The applications can only be made where there is sufficient reason and the reasons are as follows:

(a) where there is no other party on record;
(b) where no other party is affected by the order sought;
(c) where the matter is of real urgency;
(d) where secrecy prior to the application is essential for efficacy of the order.

241. Ex parte applications are generally provisional orders, and if a party objects to them, an application can be made to discharge the orders.

242. For the grant of an ex parte injunction, the requirements are set out in *Practice Direction* [1983] 1 WLR 433. The direction requires the following:

(a) that a writ of summons or draft writ of summons be prepared;
(b) there must be a summons or motion supported by an affidavit;
(c) a draft minute of the order sought be prepared.

243. The judge will examine the documents and exercise his/her discretion to grant the order.

§3. GROUNDS FOR GRANT OF AN INTERLOCUTORY INJUNCTION

244. For one to obtain an order of injunction, there must usually be a strong and clear case, as established under *American Cynamid v. Ethicon Ltd* [1976] AC 396. Lord Diplock outlined the grounds as follows:

(1) There must be a good and arguable claim to the right he/she seeks to protect.
(2) There must be a serious question to be tried though the Court must not attempt to decide the case on affidavits.
(3) The Court must exercise its discretion on the balance of convenience.

§4. GROUNDS FOR DISSOLVING AN INJUNCTION

245. An order of injunction may be discharged or vacated on the application of the defendant. The application must be supported by an affidavit and some of the grounds include:

(1) Lack of material disclosure on an ex parte application (see *R v. Kensington Tax Commissioners ex parte de Polignac* [1917] 1 KB 486).
(2) Failure of the plaintiff to comply with the terms on which the injunction was granted.
(3) Where the facts do not justify the grant of an ex parte application.
(4) Where the injunction has an oppressive effect.
(5) Where there is a material change in the circumstances of the parties.
(6) Failure of the plaintiff to prosecute the claim with dispatch.
(7) Where the injunction interferes with the life of the parties.

§5. BREACH OF AN INJUNCTION

246. Breach of an order of injunction is contempt of court punishable by imprisonment or sequestration of the assets of the contemnor, as shown in *AG v. Times Newspaper* [1991] 2 AllER 398, *Cardozo v. Mendes* cc 188 of 1978 and *Indebank v. Gredean Africa Pty Ltd* cc 1157/1993.

§6. MAREVA INJUNCTION

247. This applies where there is clear danger that a defendant may dissipate the prosperity, with the result that the plaintiff's judgment may not be satisfied. This also applies where the defendant may transfer the assets outside the jurisdiction. The application may be made before issue of writ and establishment of liability. The order prevents the transfer of assets or property, pending determination of the Court. The order derives its name from *Mareiva Compania SA v. International Bulk Carriers* [1980] 1 AllER 213.

248.   The application has to be made before a judge in chambers. This needs to be done swiftly and secretly in order to avoid the purpose being defeated. The order may be granted at any stage, even after judgment (see *Stewart Chartering Ltd v. O. Management SA* [1980] 1WLR 460).

§7.   GROUNDS FOR THE APPLICATION

249.   The application needs to be made where there exist the following grounds:

(1)   A cause of action within the jurisdiction.
(2)   A defendant must have assets within the jurisdiction.
(3)   There must be real risk that the defendant may dispose of the assets before judgment.
(4)   There must be a good and arguable case in favour of the applicant.

250.   The order may be discharged on the same reasons as those for the discharge of an interlocutory injunction.

§8.   ANTON PILLAR ORDER

251.   An Anton Pillar Order covers detention, preservation and injunction of the subject matter of the cause of action. It may be obtained where there is fear that the subject matter of the cause of action may be destroyed. The application can be made under Order 29 rule 2 of the RSC. The order derives its name from *Anton Pillar KG v. Manufacturing Process Ltd* [1976] Ch 55. The application is made ex parte before a judge.

252.   This order is draconian as it violates the defendant's rights to privacy and property hence should rarely be granted. There was little success in enforcing it in the matter of *Gwanda Chakuamba v. Attorney General and Others*[1]

> 1.   Civil Cause no. 1B of 1999 The order required that ballot papers and election materials be seized and kept till the electoral petition was concluded. The plaintiff could not enforce the order against Government due to lack of means.

§9.   GROUNDS FOR THE APPLICATION

253.   There are three grounds for the application, viz.:

(1)   There must be an extremely strong prima facie case against the defendant on the merits.

(2) The defendant's activities must cause very serious potential harm or actual harm to the Plaintiff's interests.

(3) There must be clear evidence that incriminating documents or things are in the defendants' possession and there is a real possibility that such things may be destroyed before an inter parte application.

254. The order may be discharged as any other injunction.

§10. INJUNCTIONS AGAINST THE GOVERNMENT

255. Section 10 of the Civil Procedure Suits by or Against Government or Public Officers Act cap 5:01 of the Laws of Malawi prohibits the grant of injunctions against Government or public officers. There has been debate as to whether an injunction may be granted as effective remedy in terms of section 43 of the Constitution of Malawi. However in practice, injunctions have been granted in Malawi in judicial review actions as an additional relief or stay of proceedings.

§11. INQUIRY AS TO DAMAGES

256. In cases where an injunction ought not to have been granted, for example, if the plaintiff loses a trial, the defendant may seek to enforce the undertaking in damages by applying for an inquiry as to damages. It may also occur in cases where the plaintiff withdraws the action, as seen in *Goldman Sachs International Ltd v. Lyons* (Times 28 February 1995 CA) and *Major Tsegula v. Brigadier Kadzeya.*[1]

1. Civil Cause no. 149 of 1995.

Chapter 13. Interim Payments

§1. INTERIM PAYMENTS

257. An order for interim payment may be made, requiring the defendant to pay the plaintiff where the plaintiff has admitted liability or where the plaintiff has obtained a judgment for damages to be assessed or where the plaintiff would obtain a judgment for substantial damages or where there are two or more defendants.[1] The underlying purpose is to reduce hardship or prejudice to the plaintiff with a strong claim, which may exist during the period between the commencement of the action and trial, as established under *Sherson Lehman Brothers Inc v. Madame Watson & Co Ltd* [1987] 1 WLR 480. In terms of *Shanning International Ltd v. George Wimpey International Ltd* [1989] 1WLR 981, there are three questions to be considered on an application for interim payment:

(a) Whether the plaintiff has established grounds for making an order.
(b) Whether the Court should exercise its discretion to make an order.
(c) What amount.

> 1. Order 29 Rule11 of the Rules of the Supreme Court.

258. Order 29 Rule 11 of the RSC provides that in an action for damages if the Court is satisfied:

(a) That the defendant against whom the order is sought (in this paragraph referred to as respondent) has admitted liability for the plaintiff's damages.
(b) That the plaintiff has obtained a judgment against the respondent for damages to be assessed.
(c) That if the action proceeded to trial, the plaintiff would obtain the judgment against the respondent for substantial damages, or where there are two or more defendants, against any of them; the Court may if it thinks just, and subject to paragraph 2, order the respondent to make an interim payment of such amount as it thinks just, not exceeding a recommendable proportion of the damages which in the opinion of the Court are likely to be recovered by the plaintiff, after taking into account any relevant contributory negligence and any set off, cross-claim or counterclaim on which the respondent may be entitled to rely.

259. The provision is reinforced in Order 29 Rule 12 of the RSC in case of monetary claims. The application may be made where there is an order for an account or where there is an order for possession of land, or where substantial damages may be awarded. The burden of proof is onerous on the plaintiff. The required standard is generally the civil standard, that is, proof on the balance of probabilities.

260. Order 29 Rule 11(2) of the RSC provides that in a personal injuries claim, an interim payment can be made against a defendant:

(a) who is insured against the plaintiff's claim;
(b) which is a public authority;
(c) who has sufficient means and resources.

261. The application can be granted at the Court's discretion. The application can be made by summons on ten clear days notice to the respondent.The application must be supported by an affidavit outlining the facts and grounds. The application may be continued with an application for summary judgment. At the hearing, the Court may decline granting an order for interim payment but treat the application as a summons for direction, or pre-trial review, and give directions, including ordering an early trial as to the future conduct of the action (Order 29 Rule 14 RSC).

262. The Court has the power to adjust the position of the parties after final judgment under Order 29 Rule 17 of the RSC. The Court has the power to order the plaintiff to repay all or part of an interim payment with interest, as seen in *Wardens and Commonalty of the Mystery of Mercers of the City of London v. New Hampshire Insurance Co.* [1991] 1WLR 1173.

Chapter 14. Default and Summary Judgments

§1. EARLY JUDGMENT

263. Early judgment may be obtained in default of appearance, default of defence, summary judgment or on admissions. Early judgment, simply put, means judgment without trial.

§2. JUDGMENT IN DEFAULT

264. Default judgments may be entered in two instances, viz., failure to file a notice of intention to defend and failure to file defence. Entry of default judgment is a purely administrative matter and does not involve consideration of the merits of the case at all. The procedure is aimed at preventing unnecessary expenditure of time, money and court resources in protracted litigation over undefended actions. Default judgments may be enforced but can be set aside if there is an arguable defence on the merits.

265. Judgment in default of intention to defend is only available in High Court cases where the claims endorsed on the writ are restricted to common law remedies for example:

(a) liquidated demands (Order 13 Rule 1 RSC);
(b) un-liquidated demands (Order 13 Rule 2 RSC);
(c) claims relating to the detention of goods (Order 13 Rule 3 RSC);
(d) claims for the possession of land (Order 13 Rule 4 RSC); and
(e) any combination of the above (Order 13 Rule 5 RSC).

266. A liquidated demand is an unascertainable amount of money. If the sum payable needs to be ascertained by factual investigation, then the claim is for un-liquidated damages.

§3. FILING OF DEFAULT JUDGMENT

267. The entry of judgment in default of intention to defend is purely a matter of producing the right paper work after the expiry of the time laid down by the rules. It is an administrative act. A plaintiff seeking to receive a judgment in default of intention to defend must prove two things;

(a) that the writ was duly served;
(b) that the defendant has not given notice of intention to defend.

§4. INTERLOCUTORY JUDGMENTS

268. Where the writ is endorsed with a claim against the defendant for un-liquidated damages, if the defendant fails to give notice of intention to defend after the prescribed time, the plaintiff may enter interlocutory judgment against that defendant for damages to be assessed and costs (Order 13 Rule 2 of the RSC). The damages may then be assessed in terms of Order 37 of the RSC, by the Registrar.

269. In certain cases, default judgments may not be entered without leave of the Court, for example:

(a)   where the defendant is a foreign state (Order 13 Rule 7A RSC);
(b)   where proceedings were served abroad without leave (Order 13 Rule 7B RSC);
(c)   Court actions between spouses (Order 89 Rule 2(3) RSC);
(d)   claims for specific delivery of goods (Order 13 Rule 3(1)(b) RSC); and
(e)   claims for possession of land arising out of mortgage transactions (Order 13 Rule 4 RSC).

270. Judgment may only be entered after leave has been granted by the Registrar.

§5. JUDGMENT IN DEFAULT OF PLEADINGS

271. If the defendant fails to serve the defence until fourteen days after service of the statement of claim, the plaintiff may apply to the Court for judgment in default of pleadings (see Order 19 Rule 4 RSC).

§6. SETTING ASIDE DEFAULT JUDGMENTS

272. Order 13 Rule 9 and Order 19 Rule 9 of the Rules of Supreme Court allow the courts to vary or set aside judgments entered in default.

273. The Court may act on its own motion or on application by way of summons supported by affidavit. The principle was stated by Lord Atkins in *Evans v. Bartlam* [1937] AC 473 at 480:

> The principle obviously is that unless and until the court pronounced a judgment upon the merits or by consent it is to have the power to revoke the expression of its coercive power where that has only be obtained by a failure to follow any of the rules of procedure.

§7. Irregular Judgments

274.   Irregular judgments may be set aside as of right (*White v. Weston* [1968] 2QB 677). An irregular judgment may arise in any of the following cases:

(a)   Where it is drawn as final when it should have been interlocutory for example, for damages to be assessed.
(b)   If it was entered before expiry of the time for acknowledging service.
(c)   If it was entered without leave where leave is required.
(d)   If the originating process was not served in accordance with the rules.

275.   The application needs to be made timeously see *Single v. Atenbrook* [1989] 1WLR 810 CA.

§8. Regular Judgments

276.   The Court has discretion to set aside a regular judgment (see *Evans v. Bartlam* [*supra*]). The following principles need to be followed:

(1)   Jurisdiction to set aside default judgment is not hedged by any condition and the Court should not lay down rigid rules.
(2)   The purpose behind the rules allowing setting aside default judgments is to avoid injustice.
(3)   The primary consideration is whether there is defence on the merits
(4)   The Court will take into account the defendant's explanation for allowing to be entered in default.

277.   In *Alpine Bulk Transport Co. Inc v. Saudi Eagle Shipping Co.* [1986] 2 Lloyds Rep 221, Sir Roger Omrod said that this means the defence put forth by the defendant must be one which has a real prospect of success. If there is no defence on the merits, setting aside judgment is a waste of time. If there is a defence, justice demands that it should be adjudicated upon.

§9. Summary Judgment

278.   Summary judgment is a judgment obtained without full trial, upon application to the Court. Such applications may be made where the plaintiff's case is obvious. The policy behind the procedure is to prevent delay in cases where there is no plausible defence, Lord Halsbury said in *Jacobs v. Bastics Rodrilley Co.* [1901] 85LT 262 HL:

> There are things too plain for argument and where there were defences simply for the purposes of delay which only added to the expense and where there were defences put in simply for the purposes of delay, which only added to the expense and where it was not in aid of justice that such things should continue,

summary judgment order RSC Order 14, was intended to put to end that state of things and prevent some defences from defeating the rights of parties by delay.

279.   The summary procedures include:

(a)   Summary judgment for specific performance (Order 86 RSC).
(b)   Summary proceedings for possession of land (Order 113 RSC).
(c)   Judgment on admissions (Order 27 RSC).
(d)   Summary judgment on construction of wills, contracts and documents (Order 14A RSC).

§10.   SUMMARY JUDGMENT: ORDER 14

280.   The application can be made by summons supported by affidavit after the statement of claim has been served by the defendant, on the grounds that the defendant has no defence to a claim included in the writ or to a particular part of such a claim or has no defence to such a claim or part except as to the amount of any damages claimed in terms of Order 14 Rule 1(1) RSC. Order 14 Rule 1(1) RSC precludes application for summary judgment in claims for libel, slander, false imprisonment or seduction.

281.   The preliminary requirements for the application for summary judgment include the following:

(a)   The defendant must have given a notice of intention to defend.
(b)   The statement of claim must have been served on the defendant.
(c)   The affidavit in support of application must comply with requirements of Rule 2.

282.   Rule 2 requires that the affidavit must verify the facts; and it must contain a statement of the deponents' belief that there is no defence to the claim or a part thereof in respect of which the application is made, except as to the amount of damages claimed.[1]

1.   In Civil Cause no. 2353 of 1998 *F.A Kanjala v. Norse International Limited* it was held by the Qoto Registrar that the burden of proof lay on the plaintiff to a summary judgment. In *Kasuka Mayani Properties Limited v. Kamwala Beavers Limited* Civil Cause no. 2028 of 1997, it was held that where disputed matters are not appropriate for summary judgment, they need to go for trial. In *Leasing and Finance Co. Ltd v. Murad Issa Elias t/a Crystal Waters* Civil Cause no.1808 of 1995, it was held that summary judgment under order 14 RSC would be granted where there is no dispute as to facts.

283.   The summons must be served together with a copy of the affidavit in support and any exhibits thereto not less than ten clear days before the return day. The defendant must serve the affidavit in opposition within three days before the date of hearing.

284. In terms of Order 14 Rule 3, the Court may dismiss the application or grant judgment for the plaintiff. The Court may also order a stay of execution of judgment against the defendant until after trial of any counterclaim raised by the defendant in the action.

285. The Court may also give leave to defend either conditionally or with security under Order 14 Rule 4 RSC.

286. An application for summary judgment may also be made on a counterclaim in terms of Order 14 Rule 5 of the RSC.

287. In terms of Order 14 Rule 6 RSC, the Court may give leave to defend, with directions as to the conduct of trial. The Court may sometimes treat the application for summary judgment as an application for directions under Order 111 of the Rules of the High Court.

288. A party who does not appear at the hearing of the summons may apply to have the judgment set aside or varied on such terms as the Court thinks fit in terms of Order 14 Rule 11 RSC. The rule ensures that natural justice prevails; that is, the right to be heard (*audi alteram partem*).

§11. Determination of Questions of Law Order 14A

289. The order provides that the Court may determine any question of law or construction of document arising 'without a full trial of the action' where it appears to the Court that such determination will determine the proceedings or an issue therein.[1] The Order is normally read with Order 14 as well as Order 33 on trial of issues and questions and dismissal of action after decision of preliminary issues.

  1. *Fargo Limited v. Malawi Housing Corporation* Civil Cause no. 535 of 1998, where it was held that the court would be entitled to interpret a question of law or decide on the construction of a contract.

290. Order 14A Rule 1 RSC provides

(1) The court may on application of a party or of its own motion determine any question of law and construction of any document arising in any cause or matter at any stage of the proceedings where it appears to the Court that:-
   (a) such question is suitable for determination without a full trial of action and
   (b) such determination will finally determine (subject to any possible appeal) the entire cause or matter or any claim or issue therein.
(2) Upon such determination the court may dismiss the cause or matter or make such order or judgment as it thinks fit.
(3) The court shall not determine any question under this order unless the parties have either;-
   (a) had an opportunity to be heard on the question

(b)   consented to an order or judgment or such determination.

(c)   The jurisdiction of the court under this order may be exercised by a Master.

291.   The procedure may be at the Court's instance or at the instance of the parties on application. The application may be made by summons or motion or may be made orally in the course of any interlocutory application to the Court. The requirements for employing the procedure under this order are the following:

(a)   The defendant must either have given a notice of intention to defend.

(b)   The question of law or construction is suitable for determination without trial of the action.

(c)   Such determination will be final as to the entire cause or matter or any claim or issue therein.

(d)   The parties had an opportunity for being heard on the question of law or have consented to an order or judgment being made, or such determination.

292.   The application must be supported by an affidavit deposing as to the facts on the question, order and construction to be determined by the Court. The affidavits must be sworn by the parties as the proceedings are not interlocutory.

§12.   JUDGMENT ON ADMISSIONS (ORDER 27 RSC)

293.   An admission may be by way of pleading or otherwise, in writing, under Order 27 Rule 1 RSC. Order 27 Rule 2 permits parties to actions to serve notices to admit facts not later than twenty-one days after the cause or matter set down for the purpose of the cause or matter only. Following the admission, a party may be allowed to amend the pleadings.

294.   An admission, whether made in response to a notice to admit facts or not, is not necessarily binding for all purposes. It is only binding as against the party making it, and if made under this rule, is only binding in the action including an appeal and will resemble a new trial, as seen in *Dawson v. G.C. Railway* (1919) 121 LT263. An admission in a pleading is not binding in a subsequent action (*British Turson Houston Co. v. British Insulated Helsty Cables* [1924] 1 Ch 203 at 210).

295.   Where there are admissions of fact or of part of a cause or matter either by his/her pleadings or otherwise, any other party to the cause or matter may apply to the Court for such judgment or order as upon those admissions that he/she may be entitled to, without waiting for the determination of any other question between the parties, and the Court may give such judgment, or make such order, upon application, as it thinks just, under Order 27 Rule 3 RSC. The admissions may be express or implied but they must be clear (*Ellis v. Allen* [1914] 1 Ch 904 at 909). The application may be made by motion in the action, being set down on motion for judgment, as seen in *Cook v. Heynes* (1884) WN 75.

§13. ACTIONS FOR SPECIFIC PERFORMANCE ORDER 86

296. Applications may be for specific performance in actions begun by writ, endorsed with a claim:

(a)   for specific performance of agreement (whether in writing or not) for sale, purchase, exchange, mortgage or charge for;
(b)   any property or for the grant or assignment of a lease;
(c)   of any property, with or without an alternative claim for damages;
(d)   for rescission of such an agreement; or
(e)   for failure or return of any deposit made under such an agreement; the plaintiff may, on the ground that the defendant has no defence to the action, apply to the Court for judgment. See Order 86 Rule 1(1) RSC.

297. An application may be made against the defendant under this rule, whether or not he/she has not acknowledged service of the writ in the action, under Order 86 Rule 1(2) RSC.

298. The application may be made under summons supported by an affidavit verifying the facts on which the cause of action is based and stating in the deponent's belief that there is no defence to the action. The affidavit may contain statements of information or belief, with the sources and grounds thereof. The summons must set out or have attached thereto the minutes of the judgment sought by the plaintiff under Order 86 Rule 2. The summons must be served on the defendant not less than four clear days before the return day. The summons is returnable before a Registrar.

299. The Court may give judgment or grant leave to defend in the same way it may do under Order 14 of the RSC.[1] Order 86 Rule 7 provides that judgment given in the absence of the other party may be set aside or varied.

1. *BP Malawi Ltd v. E.M. Chiume* Civil Cause no. 2052 of 2007.

Chapter 15. Interrogatories

§1. INTERROGATORIES

300. Order 26 Rule 1 of the RSC provides for discovery by way of interrogatories. By interrogation, a party may obtain discovery of facts as opposed to discovery of documents.

301. Order 26 Rule 1 RSC provides that any party to any cause or matter may serve on any other party interrogatories relating to any matter in question between the applicant and the other party in the cause or matter, which are necessary either (a) for disposing fairly of the cause or matter, or (b) for saving costs. Interrogatories may also be served with the leave of the Court. They may be served without the order and with the order of the Court. The purpose is to obtain admissions and information in advance of the trial.

302. Where interrogatories are served there must be a note at the end that the period of time for the answer is not less than twenty-eight days from the date of service in terms of Order 26 Rule 2.

303. Interrogatories without order may be served on a party not more than twice. A party on whom interrogatories without order have been served may apply to court for the interrogatories to be varied or withdrawn and the Court may make such order as it deems fit under Order 26 Rule 3 of the RSC.

§2. ORDERED INTERROGATORIES

304. These can be served where leave of the Court has been granted for service or where they are ordered to be answered, on an application under Order 26 Rule 4. The application for interrogatories may be made at the hearing of summons for directions or at any stage, but it must be supported by affidavit.

§3. PRINCIPLES

305. There is no hard and fast rule concerning the exercise of discretion to allow interrogatories, but in order to prevent abuse, a number of rules of practice have been set down and are generally followed, according to *Knapp v. Harvey* [1911] 2KB 725.

I. Relevance

306. Interrogatories must relate to the matters in question. Order 26 Rule 1. Irrelevant interrogatories are not permissible. There are three limitations

   (i)   Interrogatories going purely to the credibility of witnesses are not allowed (Order 26 Rule 1 RSC). There is need to prevent the procedure from becoming oppressive and time consuming, as seen in *Thorpe v. Chief Constable of Greater Manchester Police* [1989] 1 WLR 665, *Manica Mann George (MW) Ltd v. AGA Karim & Sons* 9 MLR 261 and *S.R. Nicholas Ltd v. Khalid Ibrahim Hasse* MSCA Civil Appeal No.6 of 1987.

  (ii) Questions can only be asked on matters relevant to the present action, not on matters that could be relevant to others on future actions (26 Rule 1 RSC).

 (iii) Fishing interrogatories are not allowed.

307.   Interrogatories must not be used in order to create a case, either for the complainant or defence (*Hennessy v. Wright* [No. 2] [1888] 24 QBD 445).

II. Facts

308.   Interrogatories must be directed at the discovery of facts. There are two limitations, viz.,:

   (i)   Interrogatories aimed at matters of opinion, especially expert opinion, are not allowed.

  (ii) Interrogatories for the purpose of discovering the evidence available to either side are inadmissible.

III. Necessary

309.   Order 26 Rule 1, provides that interrogatories are only allowed if they are necessary either for fair disposal of the action or saving costs. The rule provides for utility of the questions.

§4. OBJECTIONS AND INSUFFICIENT ANSWERS

310.   Order 26 Rule 5 permits a party to object to answer interrogatories on the grounds of privilege. However, if the answer is insufficient, the Court may require him/her to make a further answer either by affidavit or oral examination in court. It is incumbent on a party served with an insufficient answer to seek further and better particulars of the answer in terms of Order 26 Rule 5(3) of the RSC.

§5. FAILURE TO ANSWER

311.   Where a party fails to answer interrogatories or related court orders, applications can be made for the action to be dismissed or defence to be struck out, or for the party in default to be committed to prison under Order 26 Rule 6 RSC. Upon such application, the Court has the power to make such order as it thinks just, and is unlikely to use its more draconian powers except for repeated failure to comply.

The usual practice is to make an 'unless' order, providing the party in default with a final opportunity to comply before being debarred.

§6. USE AT TRIAL

312. Order 26 Rule 7 provides that answers to interrogatories may be used at the trial or may be entered in evidence and the Court is entitled to examine the answers. The answers may also be treated as formal admissions which bind the party making it.

Chapter 16. Amendment of Documents

§1. AMENDMENT

313. Changes in the parties' knowledge of a case as it progresses and straight forward drafting errors make it necessary upon occasion to make amendments to formal documents used in a case such as an originating process, pleadings, summonses, notices etc. The underlying principle is that all amendments should be made which are necessary to ensure that the real question in controversy between the parties is determined, provided such amendments can be made without causing injustice to the other party.[1]

1. *Kassam v. Lusitania Ltd* 11 MLR 248.

314. Amendments are allowed either:

(a) With the consent of the parties.
(b) In the absence of consent and without need for leave from the Court, provided the amendment is made in the early stages of the litigation and does not change the basis of the claim.
(c) With the leave of the Court.

§2. AMENDMENT BY CONSENT

315. Any pleading can be amended at any stage of the proceedings with the written consent of all the parties (Order 20 Rule 12 RSC). Unless, the parties otherwise agree or the Court otherwise directs, the costs of such an amendment are borne by the party making the amendment. Order 62 Rule (6) RSC.

§3. AMENDMENT WITHOUT LEAVE

316. The writ of summons may be amended without leave. The other forms of originating processes cannot be amended without leave at all. Order 20 Rule 1 provides that the writ of summons can be amended with limitations:

(a) The writ can only be amended on only one occasion without leave.
(b) The amendment must be made before the close of pleadings, that is, fourteen days after the services of defence or before there is a reply.
(c) Unless the amendment is made before service of writ, it must not include any change to the parties to the action or the addition or substitution of a new cause of action.

317. In *C.S. Khembo and S. Khembo v. Mandala Motors Ltd* MSCA 12 of 1984, it was held that amendments may be allowed even after closure of the plaintiff's case if no injustice would be occasioned by the amendment.

§4. ACKNOWLEDGEMENT OF SERVICE

318.   The only amendment that can be made to an acknowledgement of service form without leave is to change the statement as to whether or not it is intended to contest the proceedings. An amendment from stating no intent to defend to an intention to defend can only be made without leave, only before judgment is obtained (Order 20 Rule 2).

§5. PLEADINGS

319.   Pleadings may be amended without leave provided the amendments are made timeously. The pleadings may be amended only once without leave before the close of pleadings in terms of Order 20 Rule 3 RSC.

320.   Amendments to substitute parties or causes of action require leave of the Court in terms of Order 18 Rule 5 (2) RSC.

321.   Parties are at liberty to object to amendments without leave by applying to the Court to have amendment disallowed.The application must be made within fourteen days after the amendment in terms of Order 20 Rule 4 RSC.

§6. PRINCIPLES GOVERNING LEAVE TO AMEND

322.   The Court has power under Order 20 Rule 5 RSC, at any stage of the proceedings, to allow the amendment of any originating process, pleading or any other document in the proceedings, on such terms as that costs or otherwise may be just and in such manner if any as it may direct.

323.   In exercising this power, Bowen LJ. stated in *Cropper v. Smith* [1883] 26 Ch D 70 CA.

> it is a well established principle that the object of the courts is to describe the rights of the parties, and not to punish them for mistakes they make in the conduct of their causes by deciding otherwise than in accordance with their rights . . . it seems to me that as soon as it appears that the way in which a party has framed his case will not lead to a decision of real matter in controversy it is as much a matter of right on his part to have it corrected, if it can be done without injustice, as anything else in the case is a matter of right.

324.   In *Clarapede Co. v. Commercial Union Association* [1883] 32 WR262 Brett MR went so far as to say:

> However negligent or careless may have been the first omission and however late the proposed amendment, the amendment should be allowed if it can be

made without injustice to the other side. There is no injustice if the other party can be compensated in costs.

325.   An order for leave to amend documents may be granted in order to correct genuine mistakes.[1]

> 1. *C.S. Khembo and S. Khembo v. Mandala Motors Ltd* Civil Cause no. 12 of 1984. Amendment of a pleading will not be allowed in order to introduce an issue of fraud for the first time, *Press Agencies v. Mkwawira t/a Chimwemwe Enterprises* 8MLR 352, *Bazuka & Company v. MB Phekani & Sons* 10 MLR 332, *Ching'ande v. Musyani MSCA* Civil appeal no. 3 of 2007, which held that the court may order amendment of lists of documents, at the court's discretion.

326.   Order 20 Rule 11 gives powers to the Court to correct clerical mistakes in judgments or orders, or errors arising therein from any accidental slip or omission, at any time.[1] The application may be made by summons or motion without an appeal.

> 1. *Kayambo v. Kayambo* 13 MLR 175, where it was held that the court may only correct accidental slips but not errors of law in a judgment.

Chapter 17. Summons for Directions

§1. DIRECTIONS FOR TRIAL

327.   In Malawi, directions for trial are granted under Order 111 of the Rules of the High Court, 1981. Order 25 of the RSC is inapplicable as we have local rules.[1]

> 1.   *Limani UK Ltd v. Limani Ltd* 9MLR 329.

328.   Order 111 Rule 1 RHC provides that a summons for directions shall be taken within seven days from the date when the pleadings shall be deemed to be closed. The duty to take out a summons for directions is on the plaintiff.

329.   Order 111 Rule 2 recognizes the power of the Court to treat summons under Order 14 or Order 86 of the RSC as a summons for an order for directions.

330.   The Court has power to deal with a summons for directions in such manner as it deems fit.

331.   The Court is mandated by Order 111 Rule 2 of the Rules of the High Court to make orders as to discovery, inspection, and interrogatories, admissions of fact or documents, and place of trial. The Court may also order that particular facts be proved by affidavit or by production of documents, order a specific number of expert witnesses or indeed make any order on the pleadings as may be just.

332.   Order 111 Rule 3 provides that no affidavit shall be used on the hearing of a summons for directions. The onus is on the plaintiff to seek the directions which are practicable for his/her case under rule 4 of the Order. A subsequent application to summons for directions is also permissible under Rule 4 upon two clear days notice. However costs of subsequent applications shall be at the instance of the application by virtue of Order 111 Rule 6.

333.   Order 111 Rule 7 provides that if the plaintiff does not, within seven days from the time when pleadings shall be deemed to be closed, apply for a summons for directions under this Order, the defendant shall be at liberty to apply for an order to dismiss the action and upon such application, the Court may either dismiss the action on such terms as may be just, or may deal with such application in all respects as if it were a summons for directions under this Order.[1]

> 1.   *Dowset Engineering v. Sabadia* 11 MLR 417, *Bilji v. Electricity Supply Commission of Malawi* 8MLR 345.

Chapter 18. Discovery of Documents

§1. DISCOVERY AND INSPECTION OF DOCUMENTS

334. After the close of pleadings in actions begun by writ, there shall be discovery of the documents which are or have been in the possession of a party relating to the matters in question under the action. The parties may agree to limit or dispose with the discovery of documents, which they would otherwise be required to make to each other under Order 24 Rule 1(2) of the RSC. Discovery and inspection is governed by Order 24 of the RSC. Discovery enables parties to assess their respective cases. Documents have been defined in a broader sense. They include video tapes, films, computer diskettes or discs and databases.

335. Generally, discovery is ordered against parties to an action but it some cases it may be ordered against non-parties (see *Norwich Pharmacal Co. v. Customs & Excise* [1974] AC 133).

336. There is need for great care in the preparation of lists of documents in order to save time and costs. Discovery may be automatic or ordered by the Court. Automatic discovery occurs in writ actions within fourteen days after the close of pleadings by serving a list of documents verified by an affidavit of the documents in the possession, custody or power of a party. The list may be served, or the other party may apply to court to limit discovery for example, in personal injury claims in relation to damages.

337. Ordered discovery may be obtained on application to the Court. This normally applies to actions commenced by other modes of commencement of proceedings other than the writ. The application may be made under Order 24 Rule 3 of the RSC. The application may be granted at the discretion of the Court with a view to fairly disposing of the action or saving costs.

338. The Court may also make an order for production of the document itself under Order 24 Rule 12 of the RSC.

339. The documents subject to discovery are those within the possession, control or power of a party to the action. Power connotes that the person has a right to obtain the document from any person holding the same.

340. The documents subject to discovery must be the ones which are relevant to the action (*Campagnic Financiere v. Peruvian Guamo Co.* (1882)11QBD 55 at 63). Lord Esher permitted discovery of a document in the following manner:

> Any document which is reasonable to suppose contains information which may enable the party (applying for discovery) either to advance his own case or damage that of his opponent if it is a document which has a train of inquiry which may have either of the two consequences.

341. A legal practitioner has a duty to ensure full discovery and inspection of all documents. However the documents to be discovered must be ones which can be admissible in evidence.

§2. PRIVILEGE

342. Some documents or classes of documents are privileged from disclosure and cannot be subject to production or inspection by the other party. There are three categories of privilege, that is, legal profession privilege, self incriminatory documents, and state secrecy or public policy *(Conway v. Rimmer* [1968] AC 910, *Rush & Tompkins Ltd v. Greater London Council* [1989]AC 1280, *Ngilanzi v. Chimbende.*[1] *Construction Development Co. Ltd v. Munyenyembe*[2] and *Wangh v. British Railways Board* [1979] 2AllER 1169).

1. 10 MLR 354.
2. 12MLR 292.

343. Generally communications between client and legal practitioner are privileged. All non-prejudiced communication between the parties are also privileged from disclosure.

344. Use of documents obtained in discovery is limited to the conduct of the action only. Any misuse of the documents is contempt of court and may be protected by order of injunction or contempt of court in terms of Order 24 Rule 14 RSC.

§3. INSPECTION

345. A party who has served a list of documents has a duty to allow inspection of those documents mentioned in the list under Order 24 Rule 9 RSC. Only privileged documents are exempt from inspection. The list of documents must state the place at which the documents may be inspected and the time of the proposed inspection. If a party is failing to allow inspection, the Court may compel it to provide for inspection.

346. Order 24 Rule 11(a) allows a party to serve a notice on the party requiring the supply of copies, upon an undertaking to pay the cost of making the copies. Business books may also be inspected and entries may be supplied to the other party under Order 24 Rule 14 RSC.

347. A party is at liberty to seek specific discovery if the documents disclosed in the list are insufficient. The application may be made under Order 24 Rule 7 of the RSC by way of summons supported by an affidavit stating that there is need for discovery of specified documents and a requirement for further and better lists. The application may be made at any stage after discovery.

348.   Order 24 Rule 16 RSC provides that the Court may make an order for striking out the defence or dismissing the claim and enter a judgment for the other party, where a party has failed to comply with an order for discovery or inspection. The order may be granted upon application by the non-defaulting party.

Chapter 19. Stay of Proceedings

§1. STAY OF PROCEEDINGS

349. The proceedings may be stopped from continuing for a number of reasons and these include: mandatory mediation, arbitration clauses, pending criminal proceedings on the same issues, discontinuance or withdrawal, *forum non conviniens*.

§2. MANDATORY MEDIATION

350. Courts Act (Mandatory Mediation) Rules 2004 came into effect in 2004.The rules require mandatory mediation in all cases after close of pleadings. A matter may not proceed to hearing unless it has been referred to mediation. The rules incorporate alternative dispute resolution in civil procedure. Prior to 2004 there was no provision for mandatory mediation in civil procedure. It is aimed at having matters resolved amicably by the parties. The mandatory mediation rules are also aimed at reducing costs and delay of litigation.

351. The rules apply to all civil actions pending in the High Court and subordinate courts. In any mediation, parties need to strive to reduce cost and delay and facilitate early and fair resolution of the matter. The mediator facilitates communication between or among the parties to a dispute with a view to reaching a mutually acceptable resolution.

352. The mediator must be impartial and independent under Rule 3(2) of the Rules. A mediator may obtain expert services at the cost of the parties if they are agreeable. The mediator shall be guided by principles of objectivity, fairness and natural justice.

353. Rule 4 exempts some actions from mediation. These actions include issues of constitutional law, issues concerning liberty of the person, matters commenced under the Small Claims Procedure Rules, judicial review matters, injunctions, summary possession of land, expedited originating motion, or any expedited matter. A party to an action may also apply to the Court for exemption from mediation under Rule 4(e).

354. The mediation session needs to commence within fourteen days after the service of the defence. The session commences with the appointment of a mediator and date of the session in terms of form A. The session needs to take place within ninety days after the service of defence in terms of Rule 6(2). The mediation period may be extended for a period of not more than thirty days, under Rule 6(4). However, mediation shall be deemed to have been terminated at the expiry of the said ninety days under Subrule 2.

355.   The mediator shall be jointly chosen from a list of mediators or without such a list. In choosing mediators, parties shall be assisted by their legal practitioners. or the Court when unrepresented.

356.   Rule 9 requires that parties should prepare a mediation statement in Form B and provide a copy thereof to the other party and the mediator. The statement must identify the factual and legal issues. The material central to the case must also be attached.

357.   Mediation sessions may be attended by parties and their lawyers, under Rule 10. Parties attending a mediation session need to have authority to settle the matter or have ready means of communication with the person having authority to settle.

358.   If a party fails to attend the session without good cause, the mediator shall cancel the session and immediately file a certificate of non-compliance. In the event of a certificate of non-compliance being filed, the Court may establish a timetable for the action, strike out any document filed by a party, dismiss the action, strike out the defence, order a party to pay costs or make any order as it deems just. These powers are contained in Rule 13(2).

359.   The communication exchanged in the course of the mediation is deemed confidential and without prejudice. No party is allowed to rely on the mediation information in the proceedings. The information is privileged.

360.   On conclusion of mediation, the mediator submits a report to the Assistant Registrar (Mediation).The settlement agreement will be formulated by the mediator and signed by the parties. The signed agreement must be filed with the Court within two days from the date of signing and shall be recorded by the Court as a judgment of the Court and shall be enforced as such.

361.   If on the conclusion of mediation no settlement has been reached, then the Court shall continue with the action from the point where it was referred to mediation.

362.   A mediator may terminate where the parties execute an agreement, where the mediator cancels the session, where further mediation is difficult, where parties fail to pay deposits, where parties jointly declare that mediation is terminated or where the mediator makes a declaration to the effect that mediation is terminated. The declaration may be oral or in writing, but the mediator must record it in writing.

363.   Fees of the mediation must be equally paid by the parties unless otherwise agreed by the parties. The applicable fees are outlined in a schedule to the Rules and they range from K5000.00 to K100000.00, depending on the amount being claimed.[1] The fees may be revised by the Chief Justice.

1.   Schedule II of the Court's Act (Mandatory Mediation) Rules.

364. Rule 21 provides that there shall be no appeal against a settlement agreement filed in court after mediation.

§3. ARBITRATION CLAUSE

365. Under section 6 of the Arbitration Act[1] a party to an action may apply to court that proceedings be stayed pending the determination of the matter by arbitrators. This will normally be in pursuance to an arbitration popularly known as *Scott v. Avery Clause.*[2]

    1. Cap 6:02 of the Laws of Malawi.
    2. (1856) 5 HL Cas. 809.

366. In *Chanthunya v. Ngwira* 12MLR 133, it was held that proceedings would not continue until there was arbitration. This view was confirmed in *B.Myaba v. Commercial Assurance Union*[1] by the Malawi Supreme Court of Appeal.

    1. MSCA Civil Cause no. 23 of 1996.

367. In *Capital Investment v. Freeway Motors* Civil Cause no. 103 of 1988 (unreported), it was held that a party to an action with an arbitration clause needs to apply to court for a stay of the proceedings after filing of notice of intention to defend. The party need not take further steps in the proceedings.

§4. PENDING CRIMINAL PROCEEDINGS

368. At common law, an action for damages based on felonious acts committed against the plaintiff by the defendant is not maintainable until the criminal trial is concluded. Alternatively, a reason has to be furnished as to why prosecution has not taken place. This is known as the rule in *Smith v. Selwyn.*[1]

    1. [1914] 3 KB 98.

369. In *Chiumia v. Southern Bottlers* Civil Cause no. 707 of 1989 (unreported), it was held that a claim for damages for false imprisonment must await conclusion of criminal proceedings for theft.

370. In *Robert Construction Co. v. Yache Transport* Civil Cause no. 290 of 1980 (unreported), it was held that it is unusual to allow civil and criminal proceedings in respect of the same act to be carried on concurrently. The reason for this was that the right of the crown to the forfeiture of the felon's property might be defeated by the civil action.

371. The courts have thus granted stays on proceedings pending conclusion of criminal proceedings.

§5. Forums non Conviens

372. The High Court has jurisdiction to grant a stay on proceedings if it considers there is *forum non conviens*. In *Landell Mills Associates Ltd v. EMM Marshall* Civil Cause no. 236 of 1990, it was held that the choice of forum by the parties to a contract needs to be respected. The Court ordered a stay of proceedings on the ground of *forum non conviens* as the parties had subjected themselves to the jurisdiction of English courts by virtue of the contract.

§6. Discontinuance and Withdrawals

373. Order 21 of the RSC permits parties to litigation to drop out of the fray, usually on terms as to the payment of costs. Discontinuance is not a bar to further proceedings based on the same cause of action.

374. The Court has wide discretion to grant leave for discontinuance or withdrawal of actions on such terms as may be just.[1] Discontinuance may be made without leave where all the parties have consented in terms of Order 21 Rule 2 of the RSC. The discontinuance without leave is effected by serving all the parties with a written notice. The notice must clearly specify the action that is being withdrawn. A party served with a notice of discontinuance is entitled to lodge for taxation on a bill for the costs incurred before the receipt of the notice, unless the Court otherwise directs[2] (Order 62 Rule 5(2) RSC).

1. *Commercial Bank of Malawi v. Matomola Farm Civil Cause* no.383 of 1980.
2. *Registered Trustees of Local Transporters Association v. Tobacco Control Commission and Registered Trustees of TAMA* Civil Cause no. 128 of 2007.

375. The action may be discontinued with leave of the Court where the proceedings are so advanced that the plaintiff should not be allowed to escape contest. If leave is granted, then there should be terms as to costs or the bringing of a subsequent action in terms of Order 21 Rule 3 of the RSC.

Chapter 20. Evidence at Trial

§1. EVIDENCE

§2. EXCHANGE OF WITNESS STATEMENTS

376. Since 2005 there has evolved a practice of exchanging witness statements before trial. The practice was concretized by the Chief Justice's Practice Direction.[1] The direction states that no action will be set down for trial until witness statements have been exchanged and filed with the Court.

1. *Malawi Housing Corporation v. Komani Nyasulu* Civil appeal no. 16 of 2007.

377. The Practice Direction was made with a view to saving time and costs at the trial and to enable the parties to evaluate the merits of their dispute, with a view to settlement. Currently, the exchange of witness statements may be ordered upon the hearing of summons for directions. The rule provides for the simultaneous exchange of statements of all witnesses of fact which a party intends to call at the trial.

378. Order 38 Rule 2A of the RSC has been the basis for service of witness statements before a trial.

379. Witness statements will be part of the evidence after being adopted on oath. A witness can only be examined on the basis of the witness statement, unless with the leave of the Court, in terms of Order 38 Rule 2A (7)(b) of the RSC. The exceptions cover consent of the parties, matters outside the direction and new matters arising after service of the witness statement.

380. Similarly, cross-examination needs to dwell only on matters outlined in the statement. If there is need to cross-examine on matters not mentioned in the statement, then leave of the Court is necessary.

§3. EXPERTS

381. A person is an expert if he/she is skilled in the field in question through qualifications or experience. Experts may be called in to express opinions on matters in issue. The choice of an expert depends on the ability to pay costs.

382. Under common law, an expert was not allowed to express an opinion directly on the issues in a case.

383. Witnesses who are not experts are not entitled to give their opinions. Ordinary witnesses can only give evidence on the facts and it is up to the tribunal to draw inferences from the facts.

§4. Expert Reports

384.   There is need for disclosure of all expert reports to be used at the trial. This is to promote an open litigation policy and early settlements.

385.   In personal injury cases, the plaintiff is required to disclose the medical report substantiating the injuries at an early stage, that is, the commencement of proceedings (see Order 18 Rule 12(2A) of the RSC).

386.   At the trial the questions of admissibility of expert reports lie with the trial judge. (*Sullivan v. West Yorkshire Passenger Transport Executive* [1985] 2 All ER134 CA).

387.   Experts will give their evidence *viva voce*. Evidence will be given in chief, and it will be cross-examined and may even be re-examined. Experts may give opinions on hypothetical facts and they should give objective unbiased opinions regarding matters within their expertise. (*Polivette v. Commercial Assurance Union Co. plc* [1987] 2 Lloyds Rep.379).

388.   Issues of evidence are generally wide and they have been dealt with under various treatises, and this monograph cannot adequately address them.

Chapter 21. The Trial Process

§1. TRIAL

389. After preparations have been completed the matter must be brought before a Judge for hearing in open court. That is the trial stage. The trial may take place in chambers or in open court depending on the nature of the action.

§2. SETTING DOWN FOR TRIAL

390. After directions for trial have been given, it is necessary to prepare the case for trial and secure a date of hearing. Dates of hearing may be secured in a number of ways, and these vary with the mode of commencement of the proceedings.

§3. CASES LISTED DIRECTLY

391. Dates may give directly in some cases; for example, originating motions, petitions and expedited originating summons.

§4. INDIRECT LISTING

392. This applies to matters commenced by writs of summons. The plaintiff needs to arrange setting down of the action or the action will be struck-off for want of prosecution, in terms of Order 34 Rule 2 of the RSC.

393. Setting down has been defined as a matter of lodging bundles of documents with the Court and paying the setting down fees.

394. In Malawi, the plaintiff is expected to lodge the bundle of pleadings which include the writ of summons, the statement of claim, defence, reply to defence if any, summons for directions, certificate of a mediator and lists of documents. The second bundle to be lodged with the Court is the trial bundle which should contain the chronology of events, list of authorities, skeletal arguments and witness statements. These developments are recent. The practice has only changed since 2004.

395. The Court then arranges a setting down conference where counsel attends to the Registrar and obtains dates of hearing. Counsel agrees on the dates of hearing in terms of the directions that were given.

396. After the listing conference, the Registrar then publishes a weekly cause list. Counsel has a duty to prepare a notice of hearing and have it issued and served on the other party after a date has been given at the listing conference.

§5. ORIGINATING SUMMONS

397. Other matters commenced by way of originating summons, judicial review and petitions like divorce and electoral matters will be set down by the Registrar. Originating summons is normally set down before a motion judge responsible for chamber actions. Electoral and divorce petitions are treated as urgent matters and hence are set down by the Registrar as soon as practicable.

398. However, setting down only occurs after all the documents have been lodged with the Court.

§6. PRELIMINARY ISSUES

399. As a general rule all matters need be tried at the same time, however in some cases, costs and expenses may be served by having potentially decisive issues identified and tried separately from the main trial.

400. Under Order 33 Rule 3, the Court has the power to order three types of trials, viz.,:

(a)   trial of a preliminary issue on a point of law;
(b)   separate trial of preliminary issues or questions of fact;
(c)   separate trials of liability and quantum.

401. Order 14A also empowers the Court to determine questions of law or construction without a full trial.

§7. PROCEDURE

402. An application for a preliminary trial may be made at the summons for directions in terms of Order 111 of the Rules of the High Court, by summons to the Registrar or on application to the judge at the hearing stage. The order for preliminary trial can only be granted by the Court and not by consent of the parties.

403. In personal injuries cases there are automatic directions under Order 33 Rule 2A of the RSC for a split trial as to liability and quantum.

404. When an order for trial of a preliminary issue has been made, the Court has to formulate the issue of law or law fact to be tried. The formulation need to be done with much precision in order to avoid future difficulties of interpretation (*Allen v. Gulf Oil Refining Ltd* [1981] AC101).The Court may also order further issues to be tried on the pleadings, case stated and agreed statement of facts.

405. The House of Lords in England has condemned the practice of trying preliminary points of law without a finding on the facts as a treacherous waste of time and money in *Tiling v. Whiteman* [1979] 1AllER737.

406. The preliminary trial procedure may be employed in order to promote economy and simplicity in litigation. The invocation of the procedure is however rare.

407. In terms of Order 14A and Order 33 Rule 7, a preliminary issue which substantially disposes of the action would lead to judgment by the Court, dismissal of the action or other order as the Court may deem just.

§8. SETTING DOWN FOR TRIAL

408. Setting down of actions for trial applies only to actions begun by writ of summons in terms of Order 34 Rule 1 of the RSC.

409. Order 34 Rule 2(1) provides that the Court shall fix the date of trial of the action. In the event of the plaintiff failing to obtain a date of hearing, then the defendant is at liberty to have the action set down so that it can be dismissed.[1] In Malawi the estimated time of trial is fixed in the directions for trial, which are made under Order 111 of the Rules of the High Court.

  1. *M.F. Ahmed v. Royal Insurance Co. Ltd* Civil Cause no. 371 of 1999.

410. Where the case has not been set down after more than one year's delay there is need to give one month's notice of intention to proceed in terms of Order 3 Rule 6 of the RSC.

411. The practice in Malawi demands that in setting down an action for trial, there is need for two bundles to be lodged with the Court. The first one is the bundle of pleadings and the second is the trial bundle.

412. The bundle of pleadings contains the writ of summons, pleadings including affidavits ordered to stand as pleadings, the order for directions, lists of documents and affidavits verifying the same. This must be lodged with the Court within fourteen days after close of discovery.

413. The Court bundle or trial bundle contains the chronology of events, list of authorities, skeleton arguments, witness statements and documents to be used at the trial. This bundle must be filed fourteen days before the date of hearing by the plaintiff, in terms of Order 34 Rule 10 of the RSC.

414. However, currently the Registrar has developed a practice of setting down only actions with a trial bundle. This practice has evolved since 2004. Prior to 2004, matters would be listed for trial after a bundle of pleadings had been served. Listing of dates of trial of actions takes place before the Registrar at a listing conference in open court. Dates are allocated to matters in terms of seniority of counsel and the age of the case. Preference has generally been given to partly heard cases. The practice has led to congestion of matters on the waiting list. However there is also an attempt to amend the rules in order to promote efficiency and speedy disposal of cases.

415. The place of trial is confided to the Registry where the action was commenced that is, Principal Registry, Lilongwe District Registry, Mzuzu District Registry and Zomba District Registry. The trial may move to a *locus in quo* at any time.

§9. HEARING

416. The hearing of matters is governed by Order 35 of the RSC. The hearing is the final display of all the preparation and evidence of the case. It occurs before the judge in open court. The judge will normally sit alone without a jury. However less than half of the cases commenced in the High Court of Malawi reach trial as some are adjudged by default judgments, some by way of summary judgment, some by way of settlement by the parties even at the Court's door step and some are dismissed by reason of failure by the plaintiff to abide by the rules. The various procedural rules are intended to bring the parties to their senses and encourage them to make and accept reasonable proposals for settlement. In Malawi, the Court space is inadequate and hence the listing sessions fail to accommodate all matters awaiting a hearing.

417. Trial is aimed at determining the dispute between the parties by the judgment of the Court. Some trials are conducted so that the parties may be vindicated or so that the parties may prove the defendant's fault in public.

418. Witnesses generally attend court voluntarily, especially if they have provided witness statements. However, some witnesses do not and they have to be coerced by order of court to attend trial by way of subpoena. The evidence of expert witnesses needs to be disclosed in advance by way of expert reports.

419. Witnesses may be compelled to attend court in order to give oral evidence or to produce documents. They may be compelled by way of a *subpoena ad testificundum* or a *subpoena duces tecum*. Subpoenas may be issued administratively by way of a completed *praecipe* filed at the Registry. Conduct money need also be provided for the witnesses being compelled to attend the proceedings.

420. Evidence may also be given by way of depositions under Order 39 of the RSC. This power is exercised where the witness is over 70 years of age, too infirm to give evidence or intends to leave the country before trial. The party seeking to use a deposition may apply to the Court for an order that the witness's statement be taken down before a judge, officer or examiner of the Court. The order may also provide for examination to take place at any place, including the witness's bedside, and may provide for production of documents. There are normally the examination in chief and cross-examination in the usual way and the evidence is finally reduced to writing in the form of a deposition signed by the witness. The examiner may also report on the events of the examination.

421. Depositions are admissible at the trial if the other party has notice of an intention to have use of the same within a reasonable period in advance of the trial. It also depends on the consent of the other party or if it is proved that the deponent is dead, outside the jurisdiction, or unable to attend trial through sickness or infirmity in terms of Order 38 Rule 9 of the RSC.

422.   The persons with right of audience in the High Court of Malawi include legal practitioners and litigants in person. It is rare however that people attend proceedings in person without the aid of a legal practitioner in the High Court.[1] In the subordinate courts, most people appear in person unrepresented.

> 1. Litigants in person are generally granted legal assistance under the Legal Aid Act cap 4:01 of the Laws of Malawi.

423.   Control of proceedings at trial is the responsibility of the trial judge. The judge has a duty to ensure that the issues are identified and tried as expeditiously and inexpensively as possible. The judge may give directions as to the party to begin, the order of speeches, and may also dispense with opening speeches under Order 35 Rule 7. By *the Practice Direction (Civil Litigation: Case Management)* [1995] 1WLR 262 trial, judges are encouraged to exercise greater control over their hearings in order to reduce costs and delays. The judge may limit the length of oral submissions by counsel, the time allowed for examination and cross-examination of witnesses, the issues to be addressed and the reading aloud from documents and authorities.

424.   If the plaintiff fails to appear at the hearing, the judge may dismiss the action for want of prosecution. However if the defendant fails to attend the hearing, the Court will proceed to hear the evidence of the plaintiff and give judgment on the matter (see Order 35 Rule 1).

425.   The Court may also set aside proceedings or judgment given in the absence of the other party upon application, within seven days from the date of hearing. The setting aside is subject to order as to costs against the absent party (*Mubika v. Zimbabwe Airways* Civil Cause no. 966 of 1999).

426.   Order 35 Rule 3 also gives power to the Court to adjourn the trial of an action to any other date. Order 35/3/1 provides that an adjournment may be granted in order to save the interests of justice with regard to the following factors:

(a)   The importance of proceedings and their likely adverse effect to the party seeking the adjournment.
(b)   The risk of the party being prejudiced in the event the adjournment is refused.
(c)   The risk or disadvantage to the other party if the adjournment were granted
(d)   The convenience of the Court.
(e)   The interests of justice in general in the efficient dispatch of the delivery of justice.
(f)   The desirability of not delaying future litigants by leaving early and leaving the court room empty.
(g)   The extent to which the party seeking the adjournment has created the difficulty which had led to the adjournment see *R v. Kensington-upon - Thames Justices exp. Martin* [1994] Imm. Rep. 174.

427. Generally the power to adjourn cases is a judicial power which is exercised in the discretion of the Court.

428. The right to begin proceedings rests on the party having the burden of proof. It is generally the plaintiff who has the burden of proof and begins the proceedings in terms of Order 35 Rule 7 of the RSC in terms of *Seldon v. Davidson* [1968] 2 All ER 755.The standard of proof is proof on the balance of probabilities, which is a flexible one. Counsel will usually describe the nature of the plaintiff's case and will identify issues to be tried by reference to pleadings or skeleton argument.

429. At the trial, exhibits will be numbered and be clearly labelled as exhibits. The judge may also visit the *locus in quo* in terms of Order 35 Rule 8 of the RSC.

430. At the conclusion of the case for the plaintiff, the defendant may make a submission of no case to answer. This is considered inconvenient but the defendant may be allowed to elect whether to call for evidence or not, before making the submission (*Young v. Rank* 1950 2 KB 510 and *Kalambo v. Kumbukagha*[1]). Where the defence elects to call evidence, they may be allowed to make an opening speech and call their evidence in the same way as the plaintiff. Where there are several defendants, they call their evidence in the order they appear on the record.

1. Civil Cause no. 477 of 1996.

431. When the defence has called up its evidence, the defence's closing speech is made before that of the plaintiff. Speeches usually deal with evidence that has been adduced and the inferences that can be drawn to support the case of the party in question on the factual issues involved. Counsel will also argue any legal points that arise and sometimes make use of the skeleton arguments that have been produced.

432. The judge has a duty to maintain order in the Court and ensure that the hearing is conducted efficiently by excluding irrelevancies and preventing repetition. The judge has to press firmly but fairly to a conclusion of the matter. *Jones v. National Coal Board* [1957] 2QB55.

433. After the hearing, the judge must decide where the truth lies, decide any points of law and give judgment. Judgment is often given after an adjournment for consideration. In rare cases judgment is pronounced immediately after hearing in Malawi. There are delays in prouncement of judgments, and the time for delivery of the judgment is dependent on the individual judge. In the commercial court however, judgment must be delivered within sixty days from the date of hearing.[1]

1. High Court (Commercial Division Rules) 2007, Order 20. The Industrial Relations Court delivers judgment within twenty-one days after hearing in accordance with s. 67(4) of the Labour Relations Act cap 54:01 of the Laws of Malawi.

434. After judgment, parties may make submissions on costs but generally costs follow the event and are at the discretion of the Court. The winner at the trial will normally recover the costs

Chapter 22. Special Proceedings

§1. JUDGMENTS

435. After a judgment or order has been pronounced in court or chambers, the next step is to have it drawn up. In *Holtby v. Hodgson* (1889) 24 QBD 103 at 107, Lord Esher MR said, 'Pronouncing judgment is not entering judgment, something has to be done which will be a record.' The major distinction between judgments and orders is that judgments are final while orders are interlocutory. However both judgments and orders are enforceable in the same way.

436. Order 42 Rule 1 of the RSC provides that the judgment should be in the prescribed form.

437. Judgments must be prepared by the person having the carriage and filed in the prescribed form, and must recite the parties to the action. The name of the judge must be endorsed on the judgment. A judgment takes effect from the date of pronouncement, in terms of *Holtby v. Hodgson* (1889)24 QBD 103.It is within the powers of a judge to alter the judgment before it is entered and perfected (*Re St.Nazaire Co.*(1879) 12Ch D 88).

438. A judgment has been defined as a decision in the action and every other decision is an order (*Ex. p Chinery*(1884) 12 QBD 342.*Exp Moore* (1885) 14 QBD 627).

439. Order 42 Rule 2 provides that judgment requiring an act to be performed must specify the time within which the act must be done or some time with which the act is to be done.

440. The judge still has power to specify the time within which the money is to be paid or possession of land is to be given or goods are supposed to be delivered.

441. Judgment or order which does not specify the time within which an act is to be performed will be set aside as invalid and bad (*VanHouten v. Foodsafe Ltd* [1980] 124 SJ, 277. *Hitachi Sales v. Mitsui Osk Lines* [1986] 2 Lloyd's Rep 574 (CA)).

442. Order 42 Rule 3 provides that a judgment or order takes effect from the day of its date. Judgments or orders shall be dated as from the date of pronouncement or making, unless the Court orders it to be dated as of some other earlier day or later day, in which case it shall be dated as of that other day.

443. In *Guardian of West Ham v. Church Warders of Bethnal Green* [1895] 1QB 662, it was established that a judgment, when entered, relates back to the day on which it was pronounced.

444. Order 42 Rule 4 provides that every order of the Court shall be drawn up. These orders include orders of leave for issue and service of writs outside the jurisdiction, amendments of writs or originating processes, etc. The orders must be drawn up as soon as it is practicable.

445. It is the responsibility of the party or legal practitioner having custody of the summons, notice or other document on which an order, required by the rules of the Court to be drawn up, is endorsed. Such party is sometimes referred to as a party with the carriage of the order, and generally speaking, it is the party in whose favour an order for costs has been made who has carriage of it. If the party with the carriage fails to draw up the order then any party affected may draw up the order.

446. Order 42 Rule 5A permits the parties to enter judgment by consent. A consent judgment is an order of the Court endorsed by the legal practitioners of the parties. After a consent judgment has been drawn up it must be presented to the Court, where it will be entered or sealed like any other order or judgment. It will have the consequences of a judgment given by a judge.

§2. CORRECTION OF ERRORS IN JUDGMENTS

447. A judge who decides after giving a judgment, but before the judgment is drawn up, that the judgment is wrong, is not *functus officio*, and may recall the judgment and give a second judgment[1] (*Millenstead v. Grosvenor House (Park Lane) Ltd* [1937] 1KB 717).

1. *Kayambo v. Kayambo(supra).*

448. Order 20 Rule 11 provides that clerical mistakes in judgments or orders arising therein from any accidental slip or omission, may at any time be corrected by the Court.

449. The primary purpose of this power is akin to rectification, in that it allows the Court to correct a formal order which by accident or error does not reflect the actual decision of the judge (*Presten Banking Co v. William Allsip & Sons* [1895] 1 Ch 141).

450. However, the slip rule can never entitle the Court to reconsider a final and regular decision once it has been perfected, even if it was obtained by fraud. Further power should only be used where the amendment can be made without injustice or with terms avoiding injustice (*Lawrie v. Lees* (1881) 7 App. Cas 19 HL).

Chapter 23. Enforcement of Judgments and Stay of Judgments

§1. SPECIAL PROCEEDINGS

451. There are some proceedings or actions which are guided by special rules. These include originating summons for possession, mortgage actions, commercial matters, constitutional matters and election matters.

§2. ORIGINATING SUMMONS FOR POSSESSION

452. Order 113 of the RSC provides for a procedure for hearing of actions for possession of premises occupied by squatters or trespassers. The proceedings are commenced summarily by originating summons.

453. Order 113 Rule 1 provides that an action may be commenced by way of originating summons in cases where a person is claiming possession of land occupied without his/her license or consent.[1] The rule excludes tenants or persons occupying the land with the license or leave of the owner. Former tenants are also excluded under the rule. Order 113 Rule 1A provides that the proceedings may be heard by the master, who may refer to a judge if he/she deems it fit.

  1. *Nchima Estates Ltd v. Persons unknown, Mc Phail v. Persons unknown* [1973]3All ER395.

454. The originating summons must show whether the land in issue is residential or other land.[1]

  1. Order 113 Rule 2.

455. Order 113 Rule 3 provides that the plaintiff shall file an affidavit in support of the summons. The affidavit shall state the interest in the land, the circumstances of occupation and that he/she does not know any other person occupying the land other than those named in the summons. The affidavit shall also state the grounds for the belief.

456. The summons may be served personally on the persons named in the summons or by leaving a copy of the summons and affidavit at the premises or by sending it to the premises, or in such manner as the Court may deem fit.[1] The Court may direct that service be affected by affixing the summons and affidavit to the main door or a conspicuous part of the premises, and that stakes be placed in a conspicuous part of the land and an envelope be placed addressed to the occupiers.[2] Order 113 Rule 5 permits persons not named as parties to apply to court to join the proceedings as defendants at any stage.

  1. Order 113 Rule 4(1).
  2. Order 113 Rule 4(2).

457. A final order of possession shall be made after five clear days from the date of service in the case of residential premises and two days after service in the case of other land, in terms of Order 113 Rule 6 of the RSC. The order may be enforced by writ of possession, under Order 113 Rule 7.Order 113 Rule 8 gives the power to the Court to set aside any order that was made in the absence of the other party on such terms as may be just.

458.   This procedure is unique to squatters only.

§3. MORTGAGE ACTIONS

459.   Mortgage actions are regulated under Order 88 of the RSC. This order deals with proceedings relating to recovery of mortgaged or charged property or recovery of money due on a mortgage. Order 88 Rule 1 applies to any action by mortgage or person entitled to foreclosure or to redeem any mortgage. The relief sought may include payment of moneys secured by the mortgage, sale of the mortgaged property, foreclosure, delivery of possession, redemption, reconveyance or its release from security, and delivery of possession by the mortgagee.

460.   Order 88 Rule 3 provides that the action may be commenced by writ or originating summons. Order 8 Rule 1 of the High Court (Commercial Division) Rules 2007, provide that all mortgage actions shall be commenced in the High Court (Commercial Division).The originating summons must be accompanied by affidavit. Where the defendant does not serve an affidavit in opposition, the plaintiff must, within four days from the date of service, file a notice of appointment for hearing, in terms of Order 88 Rule 4 of the RSC. Rule 5 requires that in actions for possession of the mortgaged property, the plaintiff must show the circumstances under which the right of possession arises, the state of the account between mortgagor and mortgagee, including the amount of the advance, the amount of periodic instalments to be made, the amount of instalments in arrears or interest due and the amount remaining due under the mortgage.

461.   In actions commenced by writ of summons, judgments in default of appearance shall only be entered with leave of the Court.[1]

1.   Order 88 Rule 6.

§4. HIGH COURT (COMMERCIAL DIVISION) PROCEDURE

462.   On 3 April 2007, the Chief Justice promulgated new rules under section 67 of the Court's Act. The rules provided for the establishment of the High Court (Commercial Division) and were known as High Court (Commercial Division) Rules 2007.The overriding objective of the rules is to enable the Court to deal with commercial matters justly. The overriding objectives of the rules are outlined in Order 1 Rule 2 of the Rules as to ensure that the parties are on equal footing, saving expenses, dealing with the cases in a manner which is proportionate to the amount of money involved, the importance of the case, the complexity of issues, ensuring that matters are dealt with expeditiously and fairly and there is allotting of an

appropriate share of the Court's resources. Order 1 Rule 4 urges parties to assist the Court in the achievement of the overriding objectives.

    463. The Court has a duty to actively manage the case with a view to encouraging the parties to cooperate with each other in the conduct of the proceedings, identify issues at an early stage, decide promptly which issues need full investigation and trial and accordingly disposing summarily of the others, deciding the order in which the issues are to be resolved, encouraging the parties to use alternative dispute resolution procedure and facilitating the use of such procedure, helping the parties to settle whole or part of the case, fixing the timetable or otherwise controlling the progress of the case, considering whether the likely benefits of taking a particular procedure justify the cost of taking it, dealing with as many aspects of the case as it can on the same occasion, making use of technology and giving directions to ensure that the trial of a case proceeds quickly and efficiently. This is clear in Order 1 Rule 3.

    464. The High Court Commercial Division has exclusive jurisdiction over commercial matters.[1] Commercial matters have been defined to include a civil matter of commercial significance arising out of or connected with any relationship of a commercial or business nature, in terms of Order 1 Rule 5. Where there is doubt as to whether a matter is of a commercial nature, the judge has the power to resolve the issue of opinion and his/her decision shall be final. The value of the matters to be dealt with by the Court has been limited to not less than K1,000,000.00 (1 million kwacha).There is no limitation as regards to bankruptcy and winding up of companies.[2]

    1. Order 1 Rule 4(4) of the High Court (Commercial Division) Rules 2007.
    2. Order 1 Rule 6.

§5. Commencement of Proceedings

    465. Proceedings in the High Court (Commercial Division) may be commenced in the usual ways of writ of summons, originating summons, originating motion and petition[1] in terms of Order 2 Rule 1.Unlike in the other proceedings where the Registrar or Master has power to issue the process, in this court the judge in charge issues it and gives it the initial direction.[2] The statement of claim, as opposed to general proceedings, is known as points of claim, in terms of Order 4 Rule 1. The other unique feature of this procedure is that the writ of summons is served, together with the list of documents.[3] A reply to defence and defence to counterclaim need to be served within seven days from the date of service of the defence.[4] As soon as the defence is served the pleadings are closed and the matter will proceed to mandatory mediation in terms of rule 6 of the High Court (Commercial Division) Mandatory Mediation Rules. The date of mediation will be set by the judge within two days of the close of mediation under Order 5 Rule 6 of High Court (Commercial Division) Rules.

    1. High Court (Commercial Division) Mandatory Mediation Rules 2007.

2. Order 3 Rule 5.
3. Order 5 Rule 2.
4. Order 5 Rule3.

466. Summary judgment has been preserved under Order 7 Rule 2 for cases where there is no defence.

467. Order 11 Rule 1 provides that a judge shall fix the date of hearing of the petition at the time of issuing the process.

468. Service may be done as provided for under Orders 10,11 and 65 of the RSC, in terms of Order 12 rule of the High Court (Commercial Division) Rules.

§6. SCHEDULING CONFERENCE

469. Order 14 provides for scheduling conferences after mediation. The judge may give directions at the scheduling conference with respect to interrogatories, inspection of property, admissions of fact or documents, exchange of witness statements and place of trial, in terms of Order 14 Rule 2.The Court has powers to make such other orders as may be just. The scheduling conference is heard at the instance of the judge seized of the matter. The Court may also order filing of pre-trial check lists.

§7. PRE-TRIAL CONFERENCE

470. A Pre- trial conference shall be held not later than fourteen days from the date of hearing in order to ascertain compliance with the directions given at the scheduling conference.[1] Two days before the pre-trial conference, the parties shall lodge a pre-trial checklist. Where a party has failed to comply with any of the directions, the judge may either dismiss the action, strike out the defence or order a party to pay costs or make such other order as may be just.

1. Order 15 Rule 1.

§8. EVIDENCE

471. Order 16 Rule 1 gives power to the Court to control the giving of evidence by giving directions as to the issues it requires evidence for, the nature of evidence which it requires to decide those issues, and the way in which the evidence is to be placed before the Court. The Court may also limit cross-examination.

472. Evidence may also be given by video link under Order 16 Rule 3. The Court also has powers to make interim orders under Order 17 of the High Court

(Commercial Division) Rules. The Court has wide powers like the Court in the general division.

473. Order 18 prohibits appeals in interlocutory applications in order to avoid delaying the matter.

474. In all interlocutory matters, the parties shall file and serve skeleton arguments to be relied upon, at least two days before the hearing of the application, under Order 19. At the conclusion of the trial the parties shall file written submissions within fourteen days from the last day of trial under Order 19 Rule 2.

475. The Court shall deliver judgment within sixty days from the last day of trial.[1]

   1. Order 20 High Court Commercial Division Rules 2007.

§9. CONSTITUTIONAL PROCEEDINGS

476. The Chief Justice promulgated Courts (High Court) (Procedure on Interpretation or Application of the Constitution) Rules 2008.[1] The rules apply to proceedings on the interpretation and application of the constitution, which are certified by the Chief Justice.[2] The proceedings to be certified may involve referral actions by the President under section 89 of the Constitution, the determination of the constitutionality of an Act of Parliament or part thereof, the determination of the constitutionality of an act or omission of an organ of State or other person, a dispute between organs of State or public authorities concerning the status, powers or functions of those organs of State as provided by the Constitution, the determination of the relationship between the Constitution and a treaty or part thereof, and the enforcement and protection of the Constitution.[3]

   1. General Notice No. 20 of 2008.
   2. Rule 2.
   3. Rule 3.

477. Any proceedings shall be commenced by an originating motion within fourteen days after certification by the Chief Justice. In the case of a referral by the President then proceedings shall be commenced by way of a notice of referral. In cases of referral by other courts then the matter shall be commenced by notice of referral.[1]

   1. Rule 4.

478. Every originating summons shall be signed by the legal practitioner and shall contain a concise statement indicating the provision or provisions of the Constitution to be interpreted or applied, and sufficient particulars of the relief sought.[1] Every originating motion shall be supported by an affidavit.

   1. Rule 5.

479. A defendant who wishes to defend the whole or part of the proceedings shall within seven days of service, including the day of service, give notice of intention to defend to the Court.[1] The defendant must serve his/her concise statement of defence on the plaintiff and Attorney General within fourteen days from the date of the notice of intention to defend.[2] The plaintiff may file an affidavit in reply within seven days from the date of service of the affidavit in opposition.[3] The Registrar shall set down the matter for a pre-trial hearing conference within fourteen days of service of the affidavit in reply.[4] In case where no affidavit in opposition has been served, the registrar shall set down the matter within seven days after the expiry of the prescribed time.[5] The Court shall hear the originating motion within twenty-one days after directions have been given.[6]

1. Rule 6(1).
2. Rule 6(2).
3. Rule 6(3).
4. Rule 6(4).
5. Rule 6(5).
6. Rule 6(6).

480. Referrals by the President shall be made under section 89 of the Constitution. Such referrals shall be signed and sealed by the President. It shall also contain a concise statement of facts indicating the provision of the constitution forming the basis of the referral. The referral shall be filed with the Court for certification by the Chief Justice.[1] The Court shall within seven days of the filing of the referral cause it to be published in two daily newspapers of wide circulation and in the Gazette and place the referral at conspicuous places around the Court premises. The notice shall invite written arguments from any interested person to be filed within fourteen days from the date of the notice.[2] The registrar shall set down the matter for a pre-trial hearing conference where the Court shall give further directions for hearing, after the expiry of fourteen days.[3] The referral shall be heard within twenty one days from the date of the pre-trial hearing conference.[4]

1. Rule 7(1).
2. Rule 7(2).
3. Rule 7(3).
4. Rule 7(4).

481. A judge or magistrate or chairperson of the original court may refer any matter in relation to the application or interpretation of the Constitution within seven days from the date of the determination, to the Chief Justice for certification.[1] The proceedings in the original court will be stayed pending a decision of the Constitutional Court.[2] Where the Chief Justice has certified the matter, the Registrar shall set down the matter for a pre-trial conference within fourteen days from the date of certification. The Court shall hear the referral within twenty one days from the date of the pre-hearing conference. The decision of the Court shall be remitted back to the original court which shall decide the matter in terms of the decision of the Court.

1. Rule 8(1).
2. Rule 8(2).

482. Every originating motion shall be served personally. Personal service shall be effected by producing and leaving a copy of the document with the person to be served. Service by post is permissible. Referral by the Court shall be served by the Registrar on the parties to the original proceedings. Every process under these proceedings shall be served on the Attorney General whether or not the Attorney General is a party.[1]

    1. Rule 9.

483. The Court may admit interested persons as *amicus curae*.[1] The applicant must state before admission the interest, briefly identify the position to be taken in the matter, briefly set out the legal arguments to advanced, their relevance to the proceedings and reasons for believing that the arguments will be useful to the Court.[2] An *amicus curae* after being admitted, shall lodge written submissions within the Court on the terms and conditions determined by the Court.[3]

    1. Rule 10.
    2. Rule 11.
    3. Rule 12.

484. Judgment shall be delivered within thirty days after the conclusion of the proceedings. Every judge shall deliver judgment but a judge may elect to concur with a decision of another judge and such concurrence shall constitute a decision.[1]

    1. Rule 14.

485. These rules are a new innovation that regulate conduct of constitutional proceedings. They have been devised to promote speedy resolution of constitutional disputes. The rules are applicable in the Constitutional Court, which has a panel of three judges.

§10. ELECTION PROCEEDINGS

486. Election petitions in Malawi are held under sections 100 and 114 of the Parliamentary and Presidential Elections Act.[1] The two provisions require that a petition challenging the validity of an election be filed with the High Court. On 30 January 2009, the Chief Justice issued a Practice Direction on Abridgement of Time Periods in Election Petitions and Other Complaints under the Parliamentary and Presidential Elections Act.[2] The proceedings may relate to the electoral process or election results.

    1. Cap 2:01, Laws of Malawi.
    2. Practice Direction No. 1 of 2009.

487. The applicant will commence proceedings by way of petition accompanied with affidavit of evidence. Election results may be challenged within forty eight hours from the date results are announced.[1]

   1.   Section 100 ,Parliamentary and Presidential Elections Act.

488. After a petition has been served within seven days, the respondent or Attorney General shall file with the Court and serve on the applicant an affidavit in response with skeleton arguments.[1] Within three days of service of the affidavit in opposition the applicant shall file an affidavit in reply with skeleton arguments and serve it on the respondent or the Attorney General.[2]

   1.   Paragraph 1 of the Practice Direction.
   2.   Paragraph 2 of the Practice Direction.

489. The High Court shall hear the application within three days after the expiry of time for service of the affidavit in reply.[1] Judgment shall be delivered within fourteen days from the conclusion of the hearing.

   1.   Paragraph 3 of the Practice Direction.

490. In cases where the applicant considers a matter to be of constitutional nature under section 9(3) of the Courts Act, the Chief Justice shall certify the matter within twenty four hours of the time the notice is filed.[1] All applications for interim injunctions shall be heard inter parte before a single judge.[2]

   1.   Paragraph 5 of the Practice Direction.
   2.   Paragraph 6 of the Practice Direction.

491. Appeals from the High Court to the Supreme Court shall be heard within seven days from the date of the decision. The Supreme Court shall give its decision within seven days from the date of conclusion of the appeal hearing.[1]

   1.   Paragraph 7 of the Practice Direction.

492. The Practice Direction was promulgated to ensure expeditious and speedy disposal of electoral matters. It was also aimed at reducing certainty in the electoral process.

Chapter 24. Costs

§1. Enforcement of Judgments

493. Entering judgments per se does not provide the litigant with the remedy sought in the proceedings. Parties occasionally refuse to comply with the judgment. Public confidence in the legal system would be eroded if the Court were without powers of enforcement. There are various ways of enforcing that are designed to effect various types of judgments and these include: examination of judgment debtors, execution against goods, garnishee orders, attachment orders, insolvency, writ of possession, writ of delivery, contempt of court etc. This monograph will discuss the common methods of enforcement of judgments in Malawi.

494. The mode of enforcement of judgment is stipulated in Order 45 Rule 1 of the RSC.

§2. Execution

495. A litigant may issue a writ of *fieri facias* (*fifa*) and warrant of execution in order to enforce judgment, after a judgment for payment of money has been ordered. The writ of fifa is issued without leave of the Court and without prior notice to the defendant or other party (*Land Credit Co of Ireland v. Fermony* (1870) LR Ch 323). However, it is wrongful to issue a writ of *fifa* after payment (*Clissod v. Cratchley* [1910] 2 KB 244).

496. The writ of *fifa* is the mode of enforcement of a money judgment by the seizure and sale of the debtor's goods and chattels sufficient to satisfy the judgment and costs of execution.

497. The writ must correspond with the judgment in the names of the parties and to the subject matter of the judgment and should be directed to the proper party. In the event of discrepancies, the party responsible for the error will bear the sheriff's fees and expenses.[1]

    1. Section 44 of the Sheriff Act cap 3:05 of the Laws of Malawi.

498. The writ of *fifa* should be delivered to the sheriff for execution. In Malawi, the Sheriffs Act gives power to the Sheriff of Malawi and his/her assistants to enforce judgments.

§3. Possession of Land

499. A judgment for possession of land may be enforced by writ of possession or by sequestration, in terms of Order 45 Rule 3.

500. A writ of possession does not issue without leave except where a judgment or order was given pursuant to a mortgage action under Order 88.

501. Order 45 Rule 3(3) provides that leave shall only issue after every person in actual possession has received notice of the proceedings.

502. Under Order 113 Rule 7, a writ of possession may issue without leave of the Court. A judgment or order to give possession of land will not be enforceable by an order of committal or by writ of sequestration unless it specifies the time within which the act is to be done and if the defendant refuses or neglects to do it within that time.

§4. ENFORCEMENT FOR JUDGMENT FOR DELIVERY OF GOODS

503. Order 45 Rule 4 provides for delivery of goods ordered in a judgment. This may be enforced by writ of delivery directed at the sheriff or an order for committal or sequestration. Where there is an order for delivery, the defendant does not have the right to pay the assessed value of the goods. A writ of delivery will issue, with leave of the Court.

§5. ENFORCEMENT OF JUDGMENTS TO DO OR ABSTAIN FROM DOING AN ACT

504. Order 45 Rule 5 provides that where a person is required by a judgment or order to do an act within a time specified in the judgment or order refuses or neglects to do it within that time, or a person disobeys a judgment or order requiring him/her to abstain from doing an act, then he/she may be subjected to sequestration of his/her assets with leave of the Court. This order provides for establishing contempt of court against a defendant or a firm.

505. This rule provides for enforcement of orders of injunction whether mandatory or prohibitory.

§6. STAY OF EXECUTION

506. Order 45 Rule 11 provides that without prejudice to Order 47 Rule 1, a party against whom a judgment has been given may apply to the Court for a stay on execution of the judgment or order or other relief on the grounds of matters which have occurred since the date of judgment or order, and the Court may by order grant such relief and on such terms as it thinks just. This order gives rise to numerous daily applications before the office of Registrar. It is a useful power that may sometimes be abused.

§7. EXAMINATION OF A JUDGMENT DEBTOR

507. Under Order 7 Rule 2 of the Rules of the High Court, a judgment debtor summons may issue for examination of a judgment debtor as to his/her means. The debtor needs to be served with the summons personally and he/she is required to attend court with relevant documents. 'The examination is not only to be intended to an examination, but to be cross-examination and that of the severest in the land' per James LJ in *Republic of Costa Rica v. Stronsberg* (1880) 16 CHD 8. The basic policy is to prevent a judgment debtor defeating a judgment by dissipating or concealing assets. Accordingly, the debtor is required to answer all questions fairly directed at establishing the debtor's financial circumstances, including the amounts, names, account and policy numbers. The evidence is recorded and signed by the debtor.

508. A debtor who fails to attend may be ordered to attend at the adjourned hearing. Further, failure to attend or refusal to answer questions may result in the matter being referred to a judge for possible committal to prison.

§8. GARNISHEE

509. A garnishee has the effect of transforming a debt payable by a third party, the garnishee, to the debtor into an obligation to pay the debt to the judgment creditor. Garnishee proceedings are provided for under Order 49 of the RSC.

510. Garnishee orders generally issue against banks, building societies and creditors.

511. Firstly, the judgment creditor needs to make an ex parte application supported by an affidavit giving details of the debtor, the amount outstanding or the belief that the garnishee is indebted to the judgment debtor, in terms of Order 49 Rule 2 RSC.

512. If an order nisi has been made, it must be served personally on the garnishee at least fifteen days before the return date for an order absolute and seven days on the judgment debtor.

513. Upon service on the garnishee, the garnishee is supposed to set aside the money pending an order absolute (if the money is available) and report at the hearing of an application for an order absolute.

514. Order 49 Rule 4 provides that where the garnishee does not dispute or attend the proceedings, the Court may make an order absolute against the garnishee. An order under Order 49 Rule 4 may be enforced in the same manner as any other order for the payment of money.

515. Under Order 49 Rule 5, where there is a dispute of liability the Court may summarily determine the question at issue or order that any question necessary for determining the liability of the garnishee be tried in any manner before the master.

516. Order 49 Rule 8 provides that any payment made by a garnishee in compliance with an order absolute and any execution levied against him/her in pursuance of such an order shall be a valid discharge of his/her liability to the judgment debtor to the extent of the amount not paid.

517. In Malawi, there has been a question that a garnishee order is not effective against the Government. See *National Bank of Malawi v. Banda* Civil Cause no. 325 of 1991.[1] The debate rages on.

1. *Tayamba General Dealers v. Attorney General* Civil Cause no. 1889 of 2002 held that a garnishee order can issue against the Government. *Tratsel Supplies Ltd v. Attorney General* Civil Cause no. 676 of 2001 held to the contrary. There are conflicting High Court decisions and the position is not settled.

§9. APPOINTMENT OF RECEIVERS

518. Order 50 Rule 1 of the RSC provides that the Court may on application appoint receiver by way of equitable execution with regard to the amount claimed by the judgment creditor, to the amount likely to be obtained by the receive and to the probable outcome of his/her appointment and may directly inquire into any other matter before making an appointment.

519. Equitable execution is a process which the Court allows for the purpose of enabling a judgment creditor to obtain payment of his/her debt when the position of the real estate is such that ordinary execution will not reach it (*Wills v. Luff* (1885) 38 ChD. 197).

520. The appointment of a receiver of the interest of a judgment debtor in real estate, through sometimes by way of equitable execution, is not a mere form of execution but it is relief producing the same benefit as execution properly so-called but obtainable only by means of an order of court to that effect based on the fact that execution so called cannot be held (*re Shephard* (1890) 43 ChD 131).

521. The application for appointment of a receiver must be supported by an affidavit and it may include an application for an order of injunction.

§10. COMMITTAL (CONTEMPT OF COURT)

522. Contempt of court is punishable by way of committal to prison. Committal proceedings are governed by Order 52 of the RSC.

523. Contempt of court consists of interfering with the administration of the law (see *Attorney General v. Leveller Magazine* [1979] AC 440). It may take various forms which include:

(a) Disobedience by the contempt or if an order requiring him/her to take, or refrain from taking a specified action.
(b) Assisting another to breach such an order.
(c) Taking action which impedes or interferes with the cause of justice.

524.   The courts have insisted on the establishment of guilt and proof beyond reasonable doubt. Committal generally arises in injunctions (see *Filipo Kukhaya v. Attorney General*[1] and *Tembo and Kainja v. Attorney General.*)[2]

1. Civil Cause no.173 of 1999.
2. MSCA 27 of 2003 The case also distinguished criminal contempt from civil contempt in Malawi.

525.   However for contempt proceedings to be effective, the original order of injunction must have been personally served on the defendant, in terms of Order 45 Rule 7.

526.   Applications for committal to prison are made by notice of motion after leave has been given by the judge. The notice must be supported by an affidavit stating the grounds on which the application is made.

527.   The respondent must be served at least two clear days before the return date, unless the Court dispenses with service to do so. The hearing is before a judge in open court (Order 52 Rule 21 RSC).

528.   In Malawi, a contemnor may be imprisoned for fourteen days and subsequently up to twenty-eight days for continued contempt of court. A contemnor does not necessarily serve the entire term of imprisonment but he/she may apply to discharge the imprisonment if he/she desires to purge the contempt. The main consideration is whether the contemnor is likely to obey the Court's order in future and whether the contemnor has shown reasonable remorse (*Enfield London Borough Council v. Mahoney* [1983] 1WLR 749).The courts have also penalized the contemnors by way of fines.[1]

1. *Tembo and Kainja v. Attorney General*(*Supra*).

§11. SEQUESTRATION

529.   Like applications for committal, applications for leave to issue writ of sequestration are made by notice of motion to a judge supported by evidence on affidavit. If the contempt has been proved and sequestration is ordered for, sequestrators are appointed to enter the contemnor's lands and to seize the contemnor's personal property and to hold the same until the contempt is purged. Sequestration is common against corporate bodies.

Chapter 25. Judicial Review

§1. COSTS

530. Legal costs are incurred on behalf of a litigant from the time a legal practitioner is first consulted until the legal practitioner's retainer is terminated, perhaps after enforcement of any judgment that is obtained. The client bears the primary responsibility for paying its own legal practitioner's bill. The bill comprises the legal practitioners remuneration for the work done on the case and any export fees, court fees and any other charges expenses and disbursements. In legal proceedings, it is usual for a successful party to be awarded costs against the unsuccessful party. This reinforces the winner takes all approach of litigation. The result is that the unsuccessful litigant has to pay both his/her legal practitioner and the other party's legal practitioner orders for costs are made both at the end of trial and at the end of any interlocutory proceedings.

531. Section 30 of the Courts Act cap 3:02 of the Laws of Malawi provide:

> Subject to this Act, the costs of and incidental to all proceedings in the High Court, including the administration of estates and trusts, shall be in the discretion of the High Court and such discretion shall be exercised in accordance with the practice and procedure provided in the Rules of the Supreme Court.
>
> Provided nothing herein contained shall deprive an executor, administrative, trustee or mortgage, who has not unreasonably instituted or carried on or resisted any proceedings of any costs out of a particular estate or funds to which he would be entitled according to the rules acted upon from time to time in the Chancery Divisions of the High Court of England.

532. Section 31 provides that where the action would have been commenced in the subordinate court but was commenced in the High Court, the Court may order payment of costs on the subordinate court scale. This was affirmed in *Mario Rocha v Trustees of Dedza Diocese.*[1]

1. 11 MLR 296.

533. The fundamental principle that emerges from sections 30 and 31 of the Courts Act is that costs are in the discretion of the Court. Generally costs follow the event, that is, the successful party is entitled to recover its costs from the unsuccessful party. Order 62 of the RSC governs the awarding of costs in the High Court of Malawi. In *Singh v. Observer Ltd* [1989] 2 All ER 751, it was held that the Court has full power to determine by whom and to what extent the costs of an action are to be paid. However like any other discretion, it must of course be exercised judicially and on reasons connected with the case (*Donald Campbell & Co Ltd v. Pollock* [1927] AC 732).

534. The principles for awarding costs are outlined in *Scherer v. Counting Instruments Ltd* [1986] 1 WLR 615.

535. At the end of every interlocutory proceeding the Court may make an order as to costs. These orders are also in the discretion of the Court, in terms of Order 62 Rule 3(6) of the RSC.

§2. Costs in the Cause

536. The effect of such an order is that the party in whose favour an order for costs is made at the conclusion of the cause or matter in which proceedings in respect of which such an order would get costs.

§3. Costs Reserved

537. The party in whose favour an order for costs is made at the conclusion of the case or matter in which the proceedings arise shall be entitled to his/her costs of the proceedings in respect of which this order is made unless the Court orders otherwise.

§4. Costs in any Event

538. The order is the same as an order for costs made in interlocutory proceedings. Costs are payable regardless of the outcome of the proceedings.

§5. Costs Here and Below

539. The party in whose favour the order is made shall be entitled not only to his/her costs in respect of the proceedings in which it is made but also his/her costs of the same in any lower court.

§6. Plaintiff's Costs in the Cause or Defendants Costs in the Cause

540. The defendant or plaintiff, as the case may be, shall be entitled to his/her costs of the proceedings in respect of which an order is made, if judgment is given in his/her favour in the cause or matter in which the proceedings arise, but he/she shall not be liable to pay the costs of the other party in respect of those proceedings if judgment is given in favour of any other party or parties in the cause or matter in question.

§7. Costs Thrown Away

541. Where proceedings or any part of them have been ineffective or have been subsequently set aside, the party in whose favour this order is made shall be entitled to his/her costs of those proceedings or that part of the proceedings in respect of which it is made.

542. Order 62 Rule 3(6) defines the nature of costs to be awarded by the Court. Taxation of costs is based on an inter parte procedure.

543. Order 62 Rule 3(5) of the RSC states that where a party, by written notice and without leave, discontinues an action or counterclaim or withdraws any particular claim made by him/her against any other party, that other party shall be entitled to his/her costs of the action or counterclaim or his/her costs occasioned by the claim withdrawn, as the case may be, incurred at the time of receipt of the notice of discontinuance.

544. Order 62 Rule 9 provides for situations where costs do not follow the event. These include payment into court, offers, actions wrongly commenced in the High Court, misconduct of legal practitioner, award of nominal damages and amendment of the proceedings.

545. In the case of an order for payment into court, the Court needs to take into account any payment into court and its amount. The proper inference from this rule is that the normal result where a plaintiff fails to recover more than the amount paid in is that the plaintiff should be deprived of its costs after the date of the notice of payment. The plaintiff recovers its costs up to the date of the notice of payment into court and the defendant recovers thereafter (*Findlay Railway Executive* [1950] 2 AllER 969 CA).

546. In cases where there is an offer, the defendant would be awarded costs after the date of the offer (*Jenkins v. Hope* (1896) 1 Ch 278). Where proceedings have been wrongly commenced in the High Court, the costs awarded will be reduced in terms of section 31 of the Courts Act (see also *Mario Rocha Trustees of Dedza Diocese* (*supra*)). Where there has been misconduct by the successful party in the conduct of the proceedings costs may not follow the event (*Hobbs v. Marlowe* [1978] AC 16 HC and *Anglo-Cyprian Take Agencies Ltd v. Paphos Wine Industries Ltd* [1951] 1 All ER 873).

547. A plaintiff who has claimed substantial damages but has been awarded nominal damages will be normally be ordered to pay the defendant's costs (*Texaco Ltd v. Arco Technology Ltd* (1989), The Times 13 October 1989).

548. Order 62 Rule 6(5) provides that the cost of amendment of writ or pleadings without leave shall be borne by the party making the amendment.

549. In general, the award of costs will remain in the discretion of the court.

550. In Malawi, legal aided cases are exempted not only from filing fees but also against an award of costs in the event of failing to succeed at the trial. The exemption has arisen from extreme under-funding of the Legal Department by the Government. The exemption has come as a matter of practice which slowly has become a rule of law.[1]

1. There is a proposal by the Law Commission to have this practice legislated. See Report of the Law Commission on the Review of the Legal Aid Act, July 2005, 55.

551. The basis of taxation has been Order 62 Rule 12 of the RSC. The rule provides that upon taxation of costs on the standard basis, there shall be allowed a reasonable amount in respect of all costs reasonably incurred and any doubts by the taxing master shall be resolved in favour of the paying party.

552. Order 62 Rule 12(2) provides that on taxation on the indemnity basis, all costs shall be allowed except insofar as they are of unreasonable amount or have been unreasonably incurred, and any doubts shall be in favour of the receiving party.

553. Where there is no order as to whether the costs will be taxed on standard basis or indemnity basis, the costs shall be taxed on the standard basis, in terms of Order 62 Rule 12(1)(3).

554. In *Francis v. Francis and Dickerson* [1956] P 87, it was held that the correct view to be taken by the taxing master in considering whether any step was reasonable is that of a sensible solicitor considering what, in the light of his/her knowledge, was reasonable in the interest of his/her client.

555. Order 62 Rule 18 provides that litigants in person are also entitled to costs for work done as if it had been done by a legal practitioner, and disbursements. There is, however, a restriction on the hourly rate and rate of recovery of disbursements.

556. Order 62 Rule 19 provides that costs shall be taxed by the Registrar or Deputy Registrar or Assistant Registrar. These officers have powers similar to those of the Master in England.

557. Order 62 Rule 22 gives power to the taxing master to issue a certificate of taxation at the conclusion of taxation proceedings, issue an interim certificate or amend or cancel a certificate or correct a clerical mistake in any certificate or set aside a certificate issued by him/her.

558. Order 62 Rule 33 provides that a party dissatisfied with any decision of the taxing master may apply to the taxing master to review his/her own decision. The application for review should be made within twenty-one days from the date of the decision. The application should also contain the objections requiring review.

559. Where a party is not satisfied with the order of the master on review, he/she may seek review before a judge, in terms of Order 62 Rule 35. In the application, the party must state reasons for the review.

§8. Brief Fee

560. In *Simpson's Motor Sales (London) Ltd v. Hendon Borough Council* [1965] 1 AllER 833, Pennyquick J. stated that a proper measure for counsel's fees was to estimate what fee a hypothetical counsel, capable of conducting the case effectively, but unable or unwilling to insist on the high fees sometimes demanded by counsel of pre-eminent reputation would be content to take on the brief, but there was no precise standard of measurement and the taxing master or judge must, using their knowledge and experience to determine what was the proper figure'.

561. In *Lovedor v. Renton (No2),* preparation by counsel of his/her examination in chief and cross-examination and of his/her submissions is an ordinary part of his/her conduct of a trial on behalf of his/her client, being all part of work which counsel accepts an obligation to perform by accepting the brief and for which he/she is remunerated by the brief fee and the refreshers.

562. In Malawi, legal practitioners do claim both fees and refreshers due to the fused nature of the practice.[1] The hourly rate was defined in *Johnson v. Reed Corrugated Cases Ltd* [1992] 1AllER 169.The Court denied use of accounting knowledge and science in taxation but stated that knowledge of the taxing master and experience of local condition and circumstances was the firm basis for reliable and consistent taxation.

  1. There is a proposal to remove payment of brief fees and refreshers due to the fused nature of the legal profession in Malawi. The draft civil procedure rules have proposed abolition of these fees.

563. The approach means that in Malawi, the Registrar fixes hourly rates periodically. Currently legal practitioners with up to fifteen years experience are entitled to charge at an expense rate of K7,000.00 per hour. Those legal practitioners with more than fifteen years experience are entitled to charge K10,000.00 per hour.[1]

The expense rate was K169.00 per hour for a long time till 2004 when it was moved to K300.00 per hour. Currently there is a public perception that lawyers costs are high due to recent revision, but it is not enough compared to hourly rate charges for other professionals, that is, accountants, quantity surveyors and architects and comparable jurisdictions.

  1. Circular from Registrar of High Court of Malawi effective 1 Jan. 2004. The prevailing exchange rate is $1.00–K141.00.

564. There are also fixed costs for some works in the Courts Act.

Chapter 26. Appeal Process

§1. JUDICIAL REVIEW

565. Applications for judicial review are governed by Order 53 of the RSC. Section 16 of the Statute Law (Miscellaneous Provisions) Act cap 5:01 of the Laws of Malawi provide that the High Court has the power to grant a like order of mandamus, prohibition or certiorari. Order 53 is used in the grant of like orders. Orders of mandamus, prohibition and certiorari are granted upon issue of prerogative writs in England.

§2. THE PURPOSE OF JUDICIAL REVIEW

566. In *Council of Civil Service Unions and Others v. Minister of Civil Services* [1985] 1AC 374, it was stated by Lord Diplock that 'judicial review provides the means by which judicial control of administrative action is exercised. Its subject matter is a decision made by some person or body of persons whom I will call the decision maker or else refusal by him to make a decision'.

567. For a decision to qualify as a subject of judicial review, it must have consequences which affect some person or body of persons in either of the following ways:

(1) It alters rights or obligations of that person which are enforceable by or against which are enforceable by or against him/her in private law.
(2) Deprives him/her of some benefit or advantage which either:
  (a) he had in the past been permitted by the decision maker to enjoy and which he/she can legitimately expect to be permitted to continue to do until there has been communicated to him/her some rational grounds for withdrawing it on which he/she has been given an opportunity to comment; or
  (b) he/she has received assurance from the decision-maker which will not be withdrawn without giving an opportunity of advancing reasons for contending that they should not be withdrawn.

568. Lord Diplock's sentiments have been constitutionalized in Malawi, where section 43 of the Constitution provides the right to fair administrative justice. It guarantees the right to be heard before a decision is taken by the authorities. The remedy of judicial review is concerned with reviewing, not the merits of the decision in respect of which the application is made, but the decision making process.

569. It is important to remember that in every case, the purpose of the remedy of judicial review is to ensure that the individual is given fair treatment by the authority to which he/she has been subjected and that it is not part of that purpose to substitute the opinion of the Judiciary or of individual judges for that authority constituted by law to decide matters in question.

570. *Chief Constable of North Wales Police v. Evans* [1982] 3 AllER 14. Order 53 rule 1 provides that an application for an order of mandamus, prohibition, certiorari or injunction shall be made by way of judicial review. An injunction may be granted to a person or body, depending on the circumstances of the case.

571. Order 53 Rule 2 provides that the Court may grant any relief mentioned in Rule 1 or alternatively or in addition to any other relief.

§3. APPLICATIONS FOR LEAVE

572. Order 53 Rule 3 provides that no application for judicial review shall be made unless leave of the Court has been granted. An application for leave is made before a Judge in chambers by filing a notice in Form 86A containing a name and description of the applicant, relief sought and grounds on which the relief is sought, the name and address of legal practitioners, applicants address for service and an affidavit verifying the facts relied on. The Judge may determine the application without a hearing unless a hearing is requested in the notice of application. Hearings are always in chambers. Where the application is refused by the Judge or is granted on terms, the applicant may renew it by applying to a judge in open court. In order to renew the application for leave, there is need to file a statement in Form 86B of his/her intention to seek renewal. Under Order 53 Rule 6 RSC, the Court may allow amendment of the applicant's statement whether by specifying additional grounds or relief on the terms it deems fit.

573. Order 53 Rule 7 provides that the Court shall not grant leave unless it considers that the applicant has a sufficient interest. This rule is reinforced by section 15 of the Constitution of Malawi which provides that any person with sufficient interest may seek relief. The courts have however interpreted the provision in a varied way. In the *Registered Trustees of Public Affairs Committee* case, the Supreme Court refused to widen the scope of persons entitled to judicial review on the ground of lack of sufficient interest.[1] In *Taulo & Others v. Attorney General and Circle Plumbing Ltd* Civil Cause no. 152 of 1993, it was held that if an applicant has a direct personal interest on the relief which he/she is seeking he/she will very likely be considered as hearing sufficient interest to which the applicant relates. In this case the applicant was seeking to champion public interest in which he was not personally concerned, under the guise of applying for judicial review.

1. MSCA Civil Appeal no. 12 of 1999.

574. In *Kamuzu Banda and the Foundation of the Integrity of Creation Justice and Peace v. Attorney General* Misc Appl. 89 of 1994, the Court dismissed the second applicant due to lack of sufficient interest.

575. In *United Democratic Front v. Attorney General* Civil Cause no. 11 of 1994, the Court dismissed the action for lack of *locus standi.*

576. In *Chipeta v. Attorney General* 1504 of 1994, the Court dismissed the action for judicial review for want of *locus standi,* that is, sufficient interest on the part of the applicant.

§4. Delay in Applying for Relief

577. Order 53 Rule 4(1) provides that an application for leave to apply for judicial review shall be made promptly and in any event within three months from the date when the grounds for the application first arose, unless the Court considers that there is good reason for extending the period with which the application shall be made.

578. Order 53 Rule 4(2) provides that in the case of certiorari, the date when the grounds first arose shall be taken to be the date of judgment, order or proceedings. The rationale of the courts is to avoid public administration coming to a halt, metaphorically speaking.

579. Order 52 Rule 5 provides that where leave has been granted, judicial review proceedings shall be commenced by way of an originating motion or originating summons. The notice of motion or summons needs to be served on all interested parties within fourteen days from the grant of leave. The applicant also needs to file an affidavit of service before or on the date of hearing.

580. Order 53 Rule 6 RSC provides that copies of the statement in support of an application for leave under rule 3 must be served with the notice of motion or summons, and no other grounds shall be added apart from those set out in the summons. The Court may allow amendment at the hearing of the summons or motion, upon application.

581. Order 53 Rule 6(3) provides that a party seeking to amend his/her statement or use further affidavits, shall give notice of his/her intention and proposed amendments to every other party. Every party needs to supply the other party with copies of the affidavits to be used at the hearing. Order 53/14/6 provides that the respondent, if he wishes to rely on an affidavit, needs to file the same within fifty-six days after service on him/her of the applicant's motion.

§5. Claim for Damages

582. Order 53 Rule 7 provides that in an application for judicial review, the Court may award damages to the applicant if he/she has included a statement in support of his/her application for leave or a claim for damages arising from any matter to which the application relates. The statement for damages shall be treated as a pleading, in terms of Order 18 Rule 12 of the RSC.

§6. INTERLOCUTORY PROCEEDINGS

583. The Court (judge in chambers) may hear interlocutory applications as to discovery, interrogatories and cross-examination in terms of Order 53 Rule 8.

§7. HEARING

584. Order 53 Rule 9(1) provides that on the hearing of any motion or summons under Rule 5, any person who desires to be heard in opposition to the summons or motion, and appears to the Court to be a proper person to be heard shall be heard, notwithstanding that he/she has not been served with a notice of the motion or the summons. The Court may also order that the claim for damages shall continue to be heard as if the proceedings were begun by writ.

585. Before seeking a date of hearing, skeleton arguments need to be filed in the Court.

§8. ON WHAT GROUNDS DOES JUDICIAL REVIEW LIE?

586. This question is wide and has been adequately discussed in several texts like *Wade Administration Law*[1] etc. but there will only be a rudimentary discussion in this monograph.

   1. H.W.R. Wade & C.F. Forsyth, *Administrative Law* (Oxford: 2000).

§9. WANT OR EXCESS OF JURISDICTION

587. If an inferior court or tribunal or public authority charged with a public duty acts without jurisdiction or exceeds its jurisdiction, judicial review will lie (*Animisic Ltd v. Foreign Compensation Commission* [1969] 1AllER 208).

588. In *Benedict Nkhoma & Others v. Council of University of Malawi* MSC. Civil 154 of 1992, it was held that the actions of the faculty and senate in recommending and approving withdrawal of applicants from Malawi Polytechnic were *ultra vires*.

589. In *Du Chisiza Jr. v. Minister of Education*[1] it was held that the decision of the Minister to ban Wankhumbata Ensemble Theatre from performing in schools was *ultra vires*.

   1. Civil Cause no. 10 of 1993.

§10. Where there is an Error on the Face of the Record

590. Judicial review will lie where there is an error in the face of the record (*R v. Northumberland Compensation Appeal Tribunal* [1952] 1 KB 338).

§11. Failure to Comply with Rules of Natural Justice

591. Where the rules of natural justice apply and a decision has been reached in breach of those rules, judicial review will lie (*Ridge v. Baldwin* [1963] 2 AllER 66). In that case, a chief constable was dismissed by a police authority. The first decision to dismiss him was taken without him giving a hearing at the police authority. The Court heard that judicial review was the appropriate remedy.

592. In *Chihana v. Council of University of Malawi* MSCA 20 of 1992, the applicant was dismissed without regard to statute XV11 (c) of the University of Malawi Act and it was heard that judicial review would lie. In *Kapile & others v. Council of University of Malawi* (1992)[1] it was held that the Council of the University of Malawi had no right to expel students without a hearing. In *Nkhoma v. Council of the University of Malawi*[2] it was held that the Vice-chancellor could not validate the decision of the faculty and senate because he himself had seriously violated principles of natural justice by being part of the senate. The vice-chancellor had participated in the senate when making the decision and heard the appeal on the matter.

1. Miscellaneous Civil Application no. 47 and 48 of 1991.
2. Miscellaneous Civil Cause no. 54 of 1997.

§12. The Wednesbury Principle

593. Decisions of persons or bodies which perform public duties or functions will be liable to be quashed or otherwise dealt with by an appropriate order in judicial review proceedings where the Court concludes that the decision is such that no person or body properly directing itself on the relevant law and reasonably could have reached that decision (*Associated Provincial Picture House Ltd v. Wednesbury Corporation* [1947] 2AllER 680).

594. In *James Limbe v. Minister of Justice* MSCA Civil Appeal No. 2 of 1993, the Court held that the ban of the Malawi Democrat Newspaper was unjustified, illegal, improper, *ultra vires* and unconstitutional.

595. In any grounds for judicial review there is need for the applicant to come to court with clean hands. In *Mponda Mkandawire v. Attorney General* Misc. Civil app. no 29 of 1994, it was held that the conduct of the applicant is a relevant factor when the Court considers whether to exercise its discretion. Where the applicant behaves in an inconsiderate, defiant and provocative manner, a court in equity may refuse to grant him/her relief even if he/she establishes that the respondent unlaw-fully exercised a discretionary power.

596. In *Attorney General v. MCP, Chimango and Ntaba* MSCA Civil Appeal No 22 of 1996, the Supreme Court applied the maxim 'he who comes to equity must come with clean hands.'

§13. OUSTER OF JURISDICTION

597. In *Kondowe v. Malawi National Council of Sports* Misc. Civil Cause no. 68 of 1993, the Court held that notwithstanding Article 57 of fifa which states that National association, clubs or club members shall not be permitted to refer disputes with the Federation or other Association or club members to a court of law, and they shall agree to submit such disputes to an arbitration tribunal, even in the presence of rules which make administrative decision final the courts will intervene when the rules of natural justice are violated.

598. In *Chipingu v. Council of University of Malawi*[1] the Court found that the defendant's own rules of procedure provide that the decisions of the Appeals Com-mittee were final. Final does not preclude judicial review.

    1. Miscellaneous Civil Cause no. 5 of 1994.

§14. PUBLIC LAW ONLY IS PROTECTED BY JUDICIAL REVIEW

599. Where a person seeks to establish that a decision of a person or body infringes rights which are entitled to protection under public law, he/she must, as a general rule, proceed by way of judicial review and not by way of ordinary action whether for a declaration or injunction or otherwise (*O'Reilly v. Mackman* [1983] 2 AC 237).

600. If the person proceeds by way of ordinary action, the matter will be struck-off.

601. Sometimes the line between public and private law may be narrow: for example, in employment matters (see *O'Reilly v. Mackman*[1] and *Sawerengera v. ADMARC* Civil Cause no. 231 of 1993).

    1. [1982] 3WLR 1096.

Chapter 27. Arbitration

§1. Appeals

602. Dissatisfied litigants are entitled to appeal to higher tribunals. Appeals thus lie from magistrate courts to the High Court, Industrial Relations Court to the High Court and High Court to the Supreme Court of Appeal. Appeals ensure that errors in decisions are corrected. Appeals need to be carefully devised with regard to the Court of Appeal, leave, re-hearing or grounds of appeal.

§2. Appeals from Magistrate Courts

603. Appeals to the High Court from subordinate courts (magistrate courts) are regulated by Order XXXII of the Subordinate Court Rules. The appeal is brought by filing a notice in Form 26.

604. An appeal can be made against the whole or any part of the judgment. The notice of appeal needs to be filed within fourteen days from the date of judgment, and it must be served by the appellant on all parties directly affected by the appeal or their legal practitioners.

605. After the notice of appeal has been filed, the Court appealed against shall prepare the requisite number of the copies of record comprising the pleadings, the notes of evidence, the judgment appealed against, the documentary exhibits and any other relevant documents. The record will be prepared by the Court and served on the parties upon payment of a fee. Order XXXII Rule 21(4) provides that the appellant shall prepare a memorandum in writing setting forth the grounds of appeal within fourteen days of the receipt of the notice of appeal.

606. The High Court will then set down the date of hearing, and the appellant is expected to file skeleton arguments at least seven days before the date of hearing. The Court will then proceed to hear the matter in open court and pronounce judgment on the matter.

§3. Appeals from Decisions of the Industrial Relations Court

607. Appeals lie with the High Court of Malawi in open court. Appeals are allowed only on points of law and not on facts in terms of section 71 of the Labour Relations Act, as confirmed in *Stanbic Bank Ltd v. R.B. Mtukula.*[1]

1. MSCA 8 of 2005.

608. Upon receipt of the notice of appeal, the Court will prepare the record of appeal and forward the same to the High Court. The High Court will then set down the appeal for hearing after receipt of skeleton arguments from both parties.

§4. APPEALS FROM THE REGISTRAR (MASTER)

609. High Court (Exercise of Jurisdiction of Registrar) Rules provide:

Any person affected by any decision, order, or direction of the Registrar may appeal therefrom to a Judge at chambers. Such appeal shall be by notice in writing to attend before the Judge without a fresh summons within seven days after the decision, order of direction complained of, or such further time as may be allowed by a Judge or the Registrar. Unless otherwise ordered there shall be at least one clear day between service of the notice of appeal and the day of hearing. An appeal from the decision, order of the direction of the Registrar shall be no stay of proceedings unless so ordered by a Judge or the Registrar.

610. Prior to *Chande v. Gani,*[1] appeals on assessments of damages used to proceed to the Malawi Supreme Court of Appeal directly without going through the Judge in a chamber. The Supreme Court has since ruled that appeals against any judgment or order of the Registrar should lie with a Judge in Chambers.

1. MSCA Civil Appeal 5 of 2003.

611. Order 58 Rule 2 of the RSC provides that an appeal shall lie to a Judge in chambers against any judgment made as the decision of a Master or Registrar. The appeal shall be brought by serving on every other party to the proceedings in which the judgment, order or decision was given or made or notice to attend before the Judge on a day specified in the notice or such other day may be directed.

§5. NOTICE OF APPEAL FROM A MASTER TO JUDGE IN CHAMBERS

612. An appeal against the Master to a Judge in chambers is dealt with by way of an actual re-hearing of the application which led to the order under appeal, and the Judge treats the matter as though it came before him/her for the first time, save that the party appealing, even though the original application was not by him/her but against him/her, has the right as well as the obligation to open appeal.

613. The Judge will of course give the weight it deserves to the previous decision of the Master, but he/she is no way bound by it as per Lord *Atkin in Evans v. Bartlam* [1937] AC 473.

614. A Judge hearing an appeal against the decision of a Master however, is entitled, if he thinks fit to adopt the Master's reasoning in his own judgment, without setting out the reasoning himself, by so doing, the Judge does not fail to exercise the powers conferred on him. *Rae v Yorkshire Bank Plc.* The Times, 16 October 1989.

§6. APPEALS FROM THE HIGH COURT TO THE MALAWI SUPREME COURT

615. Hearing of Appeals in the Malawi Supreme Court is governed by the Supreme Court of Appeal Act cap 3:01 of the Laws of Malawi.

§7. APPEALS FROM DECISION OF THE JUDGE IN CHAMBERS

616. An appeal from the decision of the Judge in chambers lies to the Court of Appeal. Generally, these decisions will be in interlocutory matters, so it will usually be necessary to obtain leave to appeal.

617. Section 21 of the Malawi Supreme Court Act provides that an appeal shall lie with the Malawi Supreme Court from any judgment of the High Court in any Civil Cause or proceedings, provided no appeal shall lie against an order allowing an extension of time for appealing against a judgment, an order giving unconditional leave to defend or a judgment which is stated by any written law to be final.

618. The second provision to section 21 provides that no appeal shall lie without leave in the following cases:

(a) a judgment given by the High Court in exercise of its appellate jurisdiction.
(b) an order of the High Court made with the consent of the parties or an order as to costs only.
(c) an order made by a judge in chambers.
(d) an interlocutory order or interlocutory Judgment given by a Judge of the High Court, except in the following cases-
    (i) where the liberty of the subject or custody of infants is conceived.
    (ii) in the care of determining the claim or liability or the liability of an officer under the Companies Act.
    (iii) in the case of *decree nisi* in matrimonial causes.
    (iv) in the case of an order on a special case stated under any law relating to arbitration.
(e) an order refusing unconditional leave to defend or granting such leave conditionally.

619. The Malawi Supreme Court of Appeal has wide powers under section 22 which include:

(a) Confirm, vary around or set aside the judgment.
(b) In the interest of justice, order production of documents, order attendance of witness, receive evidence, remit the case to the High Court for further hearing and order a new trial.

620. An appeal to the Malawi Supreme Court must be filed within fourteen days for an interlocutory matter and within six weeks of the judgment in any other case, in terms of section 23. Section 23(2) gives the Supreme Court the power to extend the time for giving notice of intention to appeal.[1] Appeals against interlocutory orders need to be filed within four weeks from the date of judgment, unless leave is granted.[2]

1. *Ridgeview Investments v. Mitco Limited* MSCA Civil Appeal no. 33 of 2006.
2. *G.A. Ngosi v. Malawi Railways Limited* MSCA 34 of 2001.

§8. STAY OF EXECUTION PENDING APPEAL

621. Order 59 Rule 13 of the RSC provides that an appeal shall not operate as a stay on proceedings under the decision of the Court below, and no intermediate act or proceeding shall be indicated by appeal.

622. A successful party is entitled to enforce the judgment notwithstanding the appeal. It was held in *The Annot Lyle* (1886) 11P 116 that the Court does not make the practice of depriving successful litigants of the fruits of litigation and locking up funds to which, prima facie, he/she is entitled.

623. But the Court is likely to grant a stay where the appeal would otherwise be nugatory (*Wilson v. Church (No 2)* (1879) 12 Ch D 454) or the appellant would suffer loss which could not be compensated by damages.

624. In the case of damages, an order of stay will be granted where the appellant satisfies the Court that if the damages are paid, then there will be no reasonable prospect of recovering them in the event of the appeal succeeding (*Atkins v. Great Western Railways Co* (1886) 2 TLR 400).

625. The application for stay needs to be made before the Court of first instance and after the Court has refused them, to the Malawi Supreme Court of Appeal before a single judge, Jurisdiction of the Courts is concurrent. Such applications are held before a single judge.

626. The Malawi Supreme Court of Appeal generally has a quorum of three Judges. However in constitutional cases, the quorum is five.

627. Order 111 of the Supreme Court of Appeal provides that the appellant shall file notice and grounds of appeal stating the decision complained of, the exact nature of the relief sought and the names and addresses of all persons affected by the appeal. The notice needs be served on the respondent. The grounds of appeal need to be numbered consecutively without any argument or narrative, in terms of Order 111 Rule 2(3) of the Supreme Court of Appeal Rules.

628. Vague grounds of appeal disclosing no reasonable grounds of appeal are not permitted. Under Order 111 Rule 4 of the Supreme Court of Appeal Rules, vague grounds of appeal may be struck. The Court has the power to order amendment of the grounds of appeal under Order 111 Rule 5 of the Supreme Court of Appeal Rules.

629. Order 111 Rule 3 provides that the Court may grant leave to appeal on an ex parte motion. A party has to file a notice of appeal before the grant of leave.

630. Applications for enlargement of time for the hearing of the appeal may also be granted on good and substantial grounds outlined in an affidavit. The appellant needs to show prima facie cause as to why the appeal should be heard. When time is so enlarged,copy of the order granting such enlargement shall be annexed to the notice of appeal.

631. The notice of appeal must be served on the respondent and the respondent shall file and address of appeal for service within thirty days from the date of service of the notice.

632. The record of appeal may be settled by summons before the Registrar after the expiration of the time for filing of the address of service, in terms of Order 111 Rule 7.

633. The record of appeal contains an index, statement of the Registrar giving particulars of the case, copies of documents settled by the registrar, a copy of the notice of appeal and other documents, in terms of Order 111 Rule 9. Order 111 Rule 9 gives the responsibility of the preparation of the record of appeal to the appellant. The cost of preparation of the record is also borne by the appellant.

634. Order 111 Rule 13 gives the right to a respondent to file an intention to appeal for a cross-appeal.

635. The appellant may withdraw the appeal before appearing, and such appeal shall be deemed to have been dismissed. Under Order 111 Rule 19, after an appeal has been entered, the Court seized of the whole proceedings as between the parties shall be the Supreme Court and every application shall be made to the Court.

636. Where a party does not wish to be heard on appeal, he/she may file a submission and declare that he/she does not wish to be heard. In such a case the Court will proceed to hear the matter as if the party was heard. If the appellant fails to appear when his/her appeal is called or for hearing and has not taken any action under Rule 20, the appeal may be struck out or dismissed with or without costs. Order 21 gives power to the Court to restore a dismissed appeal, at the failure of the appellant to the cause list.

637. Under Rule 22, if the respondent has failed to attend the hearing, the Court may hear the appeal ex parte. Upon application, Rule 23 gives power to the Court to set aside the judgment given in an ex parte hearing, within twenty-one days from the date of the judgment.

638. The Court has the power to give judgment on the matter after the hearing, under Order 111 Rule 26 of the Supreme Court of Appeal Rules.

639. After judgment has been pronounced, the judgment may be enforced in the same way as a judgment of the High Court.

Chapter 28.

§1. ARBITRATION

640. The Arbitration Act cap 6:03 of the Laws of Malawi is the governing law. It was passed on 6 November 1967. Malawi is not a party to the UNICITRAL Model Law on Commercial Arbitration.

641. The Arbitration Act covers arbitration procedures and the arbitration itself.

§2. APPOINTMENT OF AN ARBITRATOR

642. An arbitrator may be appointed in terms of the arbitration agreement. Section 2 has defined the arbitration agreement as a written agreement to submit present or future differences to arbitration, whether an arbitrator is named therein or not.

643. Section 8 of the Arbitration Act recognizes the appointment of a single arbitrator by the agreement or otherwise. If there are two arbitrators, then an umpire shall be appointed in terms of section 9 of the Act.

§3. POWERS OF THE COURT

644. Section 12 of the Act gives the Court powers to appoint an arbitrator where the parties have not agreed, of if the appointed arbitrator refuses to act, or where two arbitrators fail to appoint an umpire or where the appointed arbitrator or umpire refuses to act, or dies.

§4. POWERS OF ARBITRATORS

645. An arbitrator shall have the power to call witnesses and hear them after they have been sworn.[1] The arbitrator may swear-in witnesses and subject persons failing to attend or cooperate with him/her to contempt proceedings. The Court reserves the power to order security for costs, discovery of documents and interrogatories, the giving of evidence by affidavit or examination on oath of any witnesses, preservation, interim custody or sale of any goods or securing the amount in dispute, the detention, preservation and inspection of any property under dispute, interim injunction, or the appointment of a receiver.[2]

---

1. Section 13, Arbitration Act.
2. Section13(6), Arbitration Act.

§5. MAKING OF AWARDS

646. An arbitrator may make an award at any time.[1] An arbitrator who delays in making an award or has been removed for delays shall not been entitled to fees or remuneration. An arbitrator may make an interim award in a matter. An arbitrator may order specific performance of a contract for sale, other than sale of land. An award made by an arbitrator shall be final and binding on the parties.

   1. Section14, Arbitration Act.

§6. CORRECTION OF MISTAKES

647. Section 18 of the Arbitration Act gives the arbitrator power to correct any clerical mistake or error arising from any accidental slip or omission in the award.

§7. COSTS, FEES AND INTEREST

648. An arbitrator may direct the payment of costs.[1] The costs awarded may be taxed in Court. Interest may be awarded in the same manner as in judgment debt.

   1. Section 19, Arbitration Act.

§8. SPECIAL CASES

649. An arbitrator or umpire may, if so directed by the Court, state any question of law arising in the course of reference or award or part of the award as a special case to the Court.[1] The Court has the power to decide on the special case. The Court has the power to remit awards to the arbitrator or umpire for reconsideration.[2] Upon remission, the arbitrator shall make his/her award within three months from the date of the Order.

   1. Section 22, Arbitration Act.
   2. Section 23, Arbitration Act.

§9. REMOVAL OF ARBITRATOR

650. An arbitrator or umpire who is guilty of misconduct may be removed by the Court.[1] The Court may also set aside an award where the arbitrator has proven guilty of misconduct.[2] In the event that the award has been set aside, the money payable may be paid into Court or secured otherwise, pending the determination of the application. The Court may appoint another arbitrator to replace the removed one.

   1. Section 24(1), Arbitration Act.
   2. Section 24(2), Arbitration Act.

§10. Enforcement of the Award

651.   An award made in an arbitration may, by leave of the Court, be enforced in the same manner as a judgment of the Court.[1] It may be enforced as a judgment. A litigant is thus free to issue a warrant of execution or garnishee proceedings accounts or issue committal proceedings in order to secure compliance.

1. Section 27, Arbitration Act.

Bibliography

1. Fordham, Michael. *Judicial Review Handbook.* Oxford: Hart Publishing, 2004.
2. Phiri Kings M. & another. *Democratisation in Malawi A Stocktaking.* Kachere: Zomba, 1998.
3. Jacob Jack. *Chitty and Jacob's Queen's Bench Forms.* 21st edn. London: Sweet and Maxwell, 1986.
4. J.A. Jolowicz. *On Civil Procedure.* Cambridge: Cambridge University Press, 2000.
5. Kasambara Ralph. *Cases and Materials on Civil Procedure.* 1997 (unpublished).
6. Pete Stephen & others. *Civil Procedure*: *A Practical Guide*: Icremont: New Africa Education, 2005.
7. Sime Stuart. *A Practical Approach to Civil Procedure.* London: Blackstone, 1995.
8. The Supreme Court Practice 1999 vol. 1,2 and 3.
9. Wade H.R.H. & C.F. Forsyth. *Administrative Law.* Oxford: Oxford university Press, 2000.

Statutes

10. Arbitration Act cap 6:03, Laws of Malawi.
11. Civil Procedure (Suits by or Against) Government or Public Officers Act.
12. Courts Act cap 3:02, Laws of Malawi.
13. Limitation Act cap 6 :02 Lwas of Malawi.
14. Supreme Court of Appeal Act cap 3:01 of the Laws of Malawi.
15. The Constitution of Republic of Malawi.

Abbreviations

RSC Rules of the Supreme Court
RHC Rules of the High Court
r rule
O Order
SCR Supreme Court of Appeal Rules

Bibliography

Index

Index